**COMPLETE UPDATES for IDEA 2004**

# Writing Measurable IEP Goals and Objectives

Barbara D. Bateman and Cynthia M. Herr

**IEP**

**RESOURCES**

Authors: Barbara D. Bateman, Cynthia M. Herr
Editor: Tom Kinney
Graphic Design: Sherry Pribbenow

An Attainment Publication

Second Edition

P.O. Box 930160
Verona, Wisconsin 53593-0160

Phone 800-651-0954, Fax 800.942.3865

www.AttainmentCompany.com

ISBN 1-57861-149-0

## Barbara Bateman

Barbara Bateman, Ph.D., J.D. is a nationally recognized expert in special education and in special education law. She has taught special education students in public schools and institutions, conducted research in learning disabilities, assessment, visual impairments, mental retardation, attitudes toward people with disabilities, and effective instruction for children with disabilities. She joined the faculty of the special education department at the University of Oregon in 1966 and while there also held visiting or summer appointments at several universities including the University of Virginia, the University of Maine and the University of Wisconsin.

She has authored over 100 professional articles, monographs, chapters and books. Dr. Bateman graduated from the University of Oregon School of Law in 1976, the year before the federal special education law (then called P.L. 94-142 and now known as IDEA) went into effect, and since then has worked in all 50 states, serving as a hearing officer, an expert witness, a consultant to attorneys and agencies, a speaker and a teacher of special education law. Presently, Dr. Bateman is a special education consultant in private practice.

When not writing, conducting in-service education for school districts, providing assistance to parents of children with disabilities, consulting with attorneys involved in IDEA legal actions, Dr. Bateman can be found traveling the world with binoculars and snorkel in search of birds, fish, and shells.

## Cynthia Herr

Dr. Herr is an assistant professor and Research Associate in the Department of Special Education at the University of Oregon and has been in the field of special education for 30 years. Currently, she is the program director for the Secondary Special Education Teacher Training program at the University of Oregon and has coordinated it for the past 17 years.

Dr. Herr has written and been involved in a number of federal grant projects in the area of secondary special education. She is currently the co-director of Project AIM, which trains secondary special education teachers to administer Oregon's alternate assessments, designed as alternates to required statewide tests of achievement. In addition to grant work, Dr. Herr teaches courses in the special education department including Law and Special Education.

Throughout her career, Dr. Herr has specialized in the areas of teaching students with learning disabilities and in the impact of the law on special education. Dr. Herr taught adults with learning disabilities for seven years at the community college level before beginning her career at the University of Oregon in 1985. As a consultant, she has conducted numerous workshops and made many presentations for the Oregon Association for Children and Citizens with Learning Disabilities (ACLD), the Western College Reading Association and other professional groups. She is also a certified trainer in the University of Kansas Strategies Intervention Model and has conducted in-service training for local school districts in learning strategies developed at the University of Kansas. Dr. Herr is one of the few specialists in Oregon in the area of learning disabilities assessment with adults.

In her leisure time, Dr. Herr is an avid reader of mysteries and science fiction/fantasy books and spends time with her family: A dog, a cat, and an African Grey Parrot.

Sadly, many professionals who work with Individualized Education Programs (IEPs) if given the chance, would vote to abolish them. IEPs have taken up several hundred million hours of special education personnel time (a conservative estimate) that most teachers would far rather have spent in direct teaching with students. This has to change. Society cannot, nor should it, continue to invest this much time and money with little benefit to show for it.

*Barbara Bateman*

*Cynthia Herr*

This book proposes a way to prepare the heart and soul, the nitty-gritty, the critical parts of the IEP in a way that is SIMPLE, CLEAR, USEFUL, ECONOMICAL, WORTHWHILE, COMMON 'SENSICAL,' LEGALLY CORRECT and REVOLUTIONARY. It is different from the way almost all of us have been writing **Individualized Education Program (IEP)** present levels of performance, goals and statements of service.

Sadly, many professional people who work with Individualized Education Programs (IEPs) would vote, given the chance, to abolish them. IEPs have taken up several hundred million hours (a conservative estimate) of special education personnel time that most teachers would far rather have spent in direct teaching with students. This has to change. Society cannot, nor should it, continue to invest this much time and money with little benefit to show for it.

In 1997 and again in 2004 when Congress revisited special education law (IDEA, the Individuals with Disabilities Education Act), it detailed the need for increased emphasis on measurable and measured goals, on students making genuine and measured progress, and on that student progress being regularly and meaningfully reported to parents.

This book will help every IEP team member respond effectively and without undue effort to this Congressional mandate.

However, be alerted — this is not IEP business as usual. It's much more than that. Please join us ...


*Barbara Bateman*

*Cynthia Herr*

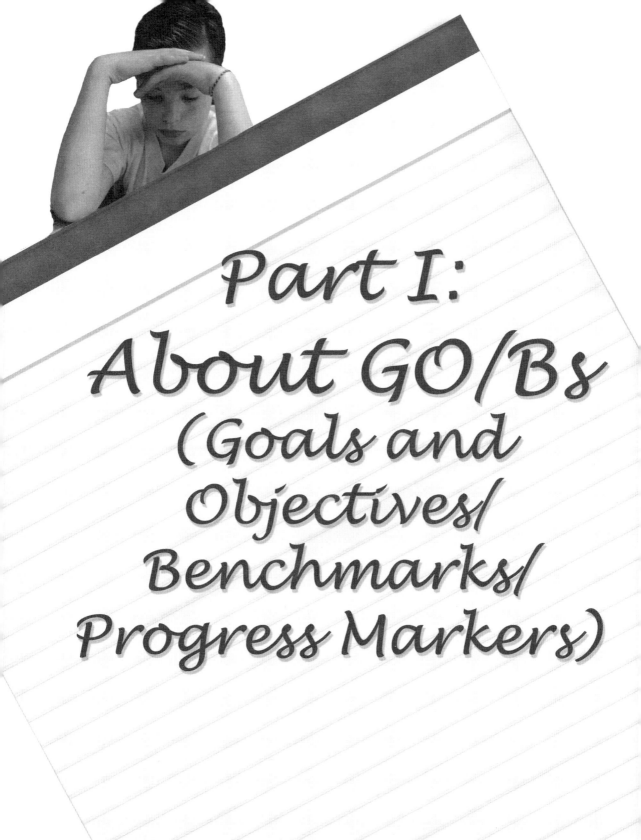

# Part I:
# About GO/Bs
## (Goals and Objectives/ Benchmarks/ Progress Markers)

# IDEA 2004

Since 1975 one federal law has guided every aspect of special education services in the United States. This law, most recently amended in 2004[1], is the Individuals with Disabilities Education Act, commonly called IDEA. IDEA provides many benefits and protections to every eligible child who has a disability, and to his or her parents. The detailed framework of IDEA provides for full and individual evaluations, independent evaluations, the provision of special education and related services, individualized placement decisions within a continuum of placement options, protections in disciplinary actions, and much more. The major purpose of IDEA is to make a free, appropriate public education (FAPE) available to every child who has a disability.

The heart of IDEA is a written document called an Individual Education Program (IEP). While all benefits and protections are important, it's the IEP process, with parents as full and equal participants with the school personnel, that determines what services the child will actually receive. These services, as spelled out in the IEP, constitute FAPE. Thus the IEP determines what happens in the child's education. The IEP is the "make or break" component in FAPE for every IDEA child.

The IEP document must include certain elements for all children plus two additional for students sixteen and older. The first three components of the IEP are key, and they are what this book is about:

1. The child's present levels of performance;

2. Measurable annual goals (and measurable benchmarks or objectives some students)[2], and

3. A statement of needed special education and other services.

Just as the IEP is the heart of IDEA, these three items are the heart of the IEP. Together, they are the key pieces of the whole law and of the child's education.

---

1. Statutory references are to IDEA 2004, regulations cited are the 1999 IDEA regulations.

2. Prior to IDEA 2004, objectives or benchmarks were required for all students. Now they are required only for certain students, as discussed below.

A three-fold inquiry determines these key pieces of the IEP:

1. What are the child's unique needs?

2. What services will the school employ to address each need?

3. What will the child be able to accomplish as a result of the services?

This three-fold inquiry translates directly into three critical elements of the IEP: The present levels of performance (PLOPs), goals, and a statement of the special education services which will move the child from the PLOP to the goal. This book is about the heart within the heart, shown in Fig. 1.

Fig. 1

*The IEP is the heart of the Individuals with Disabilities Education Act (IDEA), and measurable goals and objectives/ benchmarks/progress markers are the heart of each IEP.*

When IDEA was amended by the U.S. Congress in 1997 and even more so in 2004, new importance and emphases were placed on:

1. Special education students making more progress;

2. Special educators accurately and objectively measuring student progress; and

3. That progress being accurately and meaningfully reported to parents.

## GO/Bs Redefined

Prior to July 1, 2005, IDEA required that all annual IEP goals have measurable short-term objectives or benchmarks. Short-term objectives were defined as breaking "the skill described in the annual goal down into discrete components" while benchmarks were described as "the amount of progress the child is expected to make within specified segments of the year" (IDEA 1999 Regulations, Appendix A, Question 1).

Beginning July 1, 2005 short-term objectives or benchmarks are required only on the IEPs of those students who are assessed (under No Child Left Behind) using alternate standards rather than grade level standards. For other IEPs, short-term objectives or benchmarks are no longer mandated. However, we believe that prudent IEP teams will continue to use them for compelling educational and legal reasons.

With the new emphasis on accountability, effectiveness of the services provided, and objective progress assessment and reporting, it would be foolhardy for a school district to allow a student to fail to make progress for an entire year with no objective assessment. Furthermore, progress must still be reported to parents at least as often as it is reported to parents of non-disabled children. Even a casual reading of hearing and court decisions in IDEA cases over recent years shows that hearing officers and judges are rapidly recognizing the critical role of objectively measured progress in the education of children who have disabilities.

In addition to the huge legal risks in not objectively measuring progress at least every grading period, it is also courting educational disaster. When a child with a disability is not making adequate or appropriate progress, time is of the essence. It is unconscionable to allow a child to remain month after month in a less-than-effective program. In fact, with careful data collection, it is usually possible to determine whether a program is effective for a particular child within a few weeks. As both IDEA and No Child Left Behind push schools further toward research-based and proven interventions, we can be certain the legal and educational focus on results and outcomes, objectively measured and shown, will only increase.

The rationale of some who urged eliminating the IDEA requirement for short-term objectives or benchmarks, e.g., the Council for Exceptional Children, was the need for more instructional and preparation time for professional staff. Without in any way disputing the value of and the need for the best possible use of professionals' time, our view is that a failure to include short-term objectives or benchmarks in every IEP is short-sighted, legally risky and very poor practice. In recent years many, perhaps most, professionals involved in writing IEPs have become increasingly proficient in writing useful and measurable objectives and benchmarks. The time required to do this is a mere fraction of the value received, once a minimal level of proficiency is reached. Far more time could be saved in IEP preparation by a judicious prioritization and a limiting of goals, and by eliminating unnecessary general education curriculum and standards from all IEPs while focusing on those aspects of the child's' education that must be **individualized** and on those special education services necessary to enable the child to **access** the general curriculum. From the beginning of IDEA the federal intent has been that most IEPs be 3-5 pages long. If IEP teams examine afresh what an IEP is "supposed to be" and proceed accordingly, including objectives or benchmarks on all IEPs, far more time can be saved, with far better results than by omitting vital objectives.

The purpose of objectives and benchmarks is to assess progress. IDEA 2004 has not eliminated the requirement that progress must be measured and reported. If an IEP team chooses not to include objectives or benchmarks, it must still determine how progress will be assessed at least as often as every grading period. Hearing officers and judges are more and more frequently cautioning against reliance on subjective measures such as teacher judgment. Vague, global terms such as "emerging" or "progressing" are also rapidly becoming as unacceptable legally as they are educationally. We know of no easier, better or more efficient way to access progress than by using short-term objectives or benchmarks. The use of measurable objectives is both best educational practice and safe legal practice. To write IEPs without them is to risk a great deal for no valid reason.

To try to get by without measurable and measured progress markers is to court educational, legal and perhaps financial disaster. Without measured progress, a child may be found to have been denied FAPE. A finding that a child has not been given FAPE may be the beginning of a LEA having to pay for private schooling or provide compensatory education. However, the most important consideration is that every child should always be receiving effective services. Time is a precious commodity, never more so than for a child who needs successful intervention as soon as possible. Progress markers allow prompt action when it is needed, provided they are actually measured, i.e., the child's progress is assessed.

Throughout the discussion that follows we will occasionally use the term "progress markers" to refer to objectives or benchmarks to remind all that the function, the purpose of objectives and benchmarks is to allow us to mark progress. Progress markers, objectives and benchmarks are the same thing. A goal is just a one-year progress marker. All objectives, goals, benchmarks or progress markers must be **measurable**.

Many special educators, teachers, and other professionals experience IEPs as burdensome legal documents, laboriously completed and quickly filed — with the hope that they are never monitored and with no intention of ever using them. At the same time, many parents experience the IEP development process as intimidating, frustrating and pointless. Too often hours are spent laboring over IEP goals and objectives, and even then the results are frequently unsatisfactory, non-measurable and never-to-be-measured. However, measurable goals and objectives can be surprisingly fast, easy to write, and helpful — once the skill has been learned.

# Measurability

"Measurability" is an important ingredient in the 2004 IDEA. Before going any further, let us look at what IDEA says about measurable goals and progress reporting. The IEP must contain:

"A statement of measurable annual goals, including academic and functional goals . . . [and] a description of how the child's progress toward meeting the annual goals . . . will be measured [progress markers] and when periodic reports on the progress the child is making toward meeting the annual goals (such as through the use of quarterly or other periodic reports, concurrent with the issuance of report cards) will be provided." (20 U.S.§1414 (d)(1)(A)(i)(I, II).

The importance of this requirement for measurable annual goals and progress reporting was addressed in the 1999 Regulations. While IDEA 2004 changed the requirement somewhat, we believe the rationale is still compelling. To wit:

"Measurable annual goals, including benchmarks or short-term objectives, are critical to the strategic planning process used to develop and implement the IEP for each child with a disability. Once the IEP team has developed measurable annual goals for a child, the team:

(1) can develop strategies that will be most effective in realizing those goals, and

(2) must develop either measurable, intermediate steps (short-term objectives) or major milestones (benchmarks) that will enable parents, students, and educators to monitor progress during the year, and, if appropriate, to revise the IEP consistent with student instructional needs.

As noted, each annual goal must include either short-term objectives or benchmarks. The purpose of both is to enable a child's teachers, parents, and others involved in developing and implementing the child's IEP, to gauge, at intermediate times during the year, how well the child is progressing toward achievement of the annual goal. IEP teams may continue to develop short-term instructional objectives that generally break the skills (described in the annual goal) down into discrete components. The revised statute and regulations also provide that, as an alternative, IEP teams may develop benchmarks which describe the amount of progress the child is expected to make within specified segments of the year. Generally, benchmarks establish expected performance levels that allow for regular checks of progress that coincide with the reporting periods for informing parents of their child's progress toward achieving the annual goals. An IEP team may use short term objectives, benchmarks or a combination of the two, depending on the nature of annual goals and needs of the child." (Appendix A, 1999 IDEA Regulations, Question 1.)

IDEA leaves no doubt that measurability is both mandated and absolutely essential. Without measurability, progress cannot be monitored. However, measurability alone is not sufficient. Goals and objectives must be both **measurable and measured** in order to determine progress and to make necessary revisions to the IEP.

*All goals and progress markers must be measurable and measured.*

What exactly does measurable mean? Unfortunately, IDEA doesn't define it for us. So, we will examine measurability and non-measurability, as well as look closely at other important terms.

# Measurable

"Measurable" is the essential characteristic of an IEP goal or objective. When a goal isn't measurable, it cannot be measured. If it cannot be measured, it violates IDEA and may result in a denial of FAPE to the child.

*To measure is to do something.*

To measure something is to perform a particular operation, **to do** something. To measure one's weight, stand on a scale. To measure temperature, look at a thermometer. To measure tire pressure, put a gauge on the valve stem. And so on. To measure is to perform an action of some type. An important question to keep in mind when writing measurable GO/Bs is, "What would one do to see if the child has accomplished this GO/B?"

Another key consideration is whether, if several people evaluated the student's performance, they would come to the same conclusion about accomplishment of the GO/B.

*Multiple evaluators can agree on whether the student has reached the goal.*

If the goal were that Rocky would learn "to cope appropriately with being teased," evaluators could easily disagree whether certain responses demonstrated appropriate coping. If the goal were, "When teased, Rocky would make no verbal response and would walk away," observers would be likely to agree.

A third issue is that when the GO/B is measured, we must be able to say **how much** progress has been made since the PLOP or previous GO/B was measured. "How much" requires some degree or level of quantification. This is not to say we must insert 80% (or any other %) into every GO/B! Doing that routinely, as many people do, has some sad and some absurd results, as we'll see later.

One further characteristic of a measurable GO/B is that it can be measured as it is written, without having to refer to additional, external information. Whether a student can "count to 10 without error" can be readily determined as it is stated. But "will improve counting skill" cannot

> *A measurable goal allows us to know how much progress has been made since the last measured performance.*

be assessed without additional information about the previous counting skill level. It also fails to indicate how much improvement (i.e., to what level), will satisfy the goal. In sum, a measurable GO/B:

1. Reveals what to do to measure whether the GO/B has been accomplished;

2. Yields the same conclusion if measured by several people;

> *A measurable goal can be measured as written, without additional information.*

3. Allows a calculation of how much progress it represents; and

4. Can be measured without additional information.

These four characteristics describe measurability. In addition, a measurable GO/B contains (1) an observable learner performance (what the learner will be doing, such as counting, writing, pointing, describing, etc.), (2) any important conditions such as "given software," or "given access to a dictionary," and (3) measurable criteria which specify the level at which the student's performance will be acceptable (e.g., speed, accuracy, frequency, quality).

If a GO/B contains a given or condition, the given is usually stated first. The learner's performance is stated next, and the desired level of performance or criteria is stated last. Notice that in these four examples, two contain givens and two don't:

1. Given 2nd grade material, Jerry will read orally at 60 wpm with no more than 2 errors.

2. Jeremy will tantrum less than 5 minutes per week.

> *Measurable goals and objectives contain givens (if necessary), the learner performance, and the criterion (level of performance to be reached).*

3. Given a 15 minute recess period, Jason will appropriately initiate interaction with at least one peer.

4. Jonathan will copy 20 letters per minute with all legible.

Before going any further, we suggest you examine these GO/Bs to see if each satisfies our four indicators of measurability and if you can identify the given (if present), the learner performance, and the criterion or level of expected performance. Now we need to look more closely at each element of a measurable GO/B — the given, the performance and the criterion.

## Givens

Goals sometimes require a statement of a given and sometimes don't. Common sense is the guide, as shown in these examples:

A **given** is needed:

Given access to the Internet, student will locate ten sources of information on topic X. (Without the Internet, it would be a different GO/B.)

A given is **not** needed:

The student will bounce to a height of one foot, five consecutive times without falling off a trampoline. (The 'given' trampoline is imbedded).

A **given** is needed:

Given a calculator, the student will correctly solve ten 3-digit x 2-digit multiplication problems in one minute. (Without the given, it becomes a different, but also completely legitimate task.)

A given is **not** needed:

The student will swim 200 yards in X time without stopping, using two strokes of her choice. (We can assume the presence of water.)

Common sense is the best guide for when a given needs to be stated explicitly. If the goal is that Joe zips his trousers on 10 consecutive trials, we can assume he has trousers that zip. Don't put conditions that aren't needed and never use "instruction" as a given. It is always an assumed given – if the student could already perform it without instruction, it wouldn't be a legitimate or appropriate goal.

## Learner's Performance/Behavior

Often, the most problematic element of measurable goals for many of us to acquire or grasp is the **observable**, **visible** or **countable behavior**. Here are some examples of observable, and not observable behaviors:

| Observable | Not Observable |
|---|---|
| matching author to book title | appreciating art |
| reading orally | enjoying literature |
| constructing a time line | understanding history |
| dressing one's self | becoming independent |
| speaking to adults without vulgarities | respecting authority |
| pointing, drawing, identifying, writing, etc. | improving, feeling, knowing |

Of course, we hope our students will appreciate, enjoy, understand, respect and more. Of that there is no doubt. But for purposes of measurable progress markers, we must ask ourselves what we hope to see, the visible behavior, that we'll accept as indicating that our student is appreciating nature, enjoying literature, or being respectful to adults.

## Criterion or Level of Performance

The criterion is simply how well the learner must do — the level of performance required — to meet the goal. To say we want Becky "to identify (name) colors" is not sufficient. If she named only red and blue, would that satisfy the goal? Does she need to name puce and mauve?

A graduate school once specified that one criterion to earn a Ph.D. was to have a professional article "accepted for publication in a refereed journal." The criterion is the height to which the performance must rise, or the depth to which it must fall (if digging a 3' deep post hole) to be successful. Frequently used criteria include 4 of 5 trials, 3 consecutive days, once a day, etc. The most abused criterion, beyond a doubt, is percentage. For example, Benny will "use three anger management skills with 80% accuracy," or Kenny will "maintain appropriate eye contact with 90% accuracy." What good will it do Benny to use three anger management skills

*The history of how this strange use of percentage began appears to be lost. But we should know not to aspire to have Josh "cross the street safely 80% of the time."*

partially correct? How will you measure whether Kenny maintains eye contact with 90% accuracy (what is accuracy when it comes to eye contact)? The history of how this strange use of percentage began appears to be lost, but we now must bury the custom. It makes good sense to say Katy will perform 2 digit by 1 digit multiplication problems with 98% accuracy, or she will correctly spell 95% of the 6th grade spelling words dictated to her. However, the use of percentage needs to be carefully limited to a narrow range of goals. Never again should Don be requested to "improve his behavior with 75% accuracy," nor Annabel be required to "improve her behavior 80% of the time." And most especially, we should not aspire to have Josh "cross the street safely 80% of the time."

*Some goals are 100% non-measurable and useless, e.g., "Jane will improve her behavior 80% of the time with 90% accuracy."*

## Non-Measurable

Just as measurability is so essential that it must be achieved in every useful, legally correct GO/B, so non-measurability must be diligently avoided. Unfortunately, many IEPs offer abundant examples of non-measurable GO/Bs.

Some examples, all from real IEPs, follow.

*"Rebecca will increase her active listening skills."*

This GO/B has no criterion to indicate the level at which Rebecca must perform to reach the goal, nor does it specify the behavior of "active listening." If two or more people tried to see if Rebecca had accomplished this, they might well disagree with each other. Even if we knew what this goal writer meant by "active listening skills," we could not tell if Rebecca had "improved" without knowing the previous level of her skills. Thousands and thousands of goals use this "student will improve X" format. It is not measurable, not acceptable and not useful. To improve this goal, we must ask what the writer meant. What might Rebecca do that would make us think she is "actively listening?" Perhaps "following oral directions" would be an acceptable, visible learner performance. This **measurable** version is probably closer to what was intended: "Given 5 simple, two-step oral directions such as, 'Fold your paper and hand it in,' Rebecca will correctly complete 4 of the 5 two-step directions."

*"Tammy will increase basic and other life skills."*

This goal suffers exactly as did Rebecca's, i.e., "increase," like "improve," requires additional information about previous levels of performance. "Basic and other life skills" is even broader and more vague than "active listening skills." This goal, in short, has no visible learner performance and no criterion for performance. Thus it, like Rebecca's, is not measurable, useful nor compliant with IDEA's mandate. What might this goal writer have intended? Literally, hundreds of behaviors could have been meant by "basic and other life skills," ranging from independent toileting or teeth brushing, to dressing, using the Internet, shopping, or budgeting. Any effort to translate Tammy's goal into a measurable one would be a guessing game. This goal writer didn't give us even one helpful clue.

*"Kevin will decrease his inappropriate remarks to other children 90% of the time."*

"Decrease his inappropriate remarks" is indeed a visible learner performance, but what in the world is "90% of the time?" This is gibberish. Suppose Kevin makes an average of 10 inappropriate remarks daily. Presumably this gibberish writer intended to reduce that by 90 percent, i.e., to have Kevin make no more than one inappropriate remark daily. If so, that is exactly what should have been said: Kevin will make no more than one inappropriate remark to other children daily.

Granted, "inappropriate" is a wee bit vague and could lead to an occasional difference of opinion among evaluators. Nevertheless, it is well within the boundaries we're comfortable with in our real world.

*"Max will be 75% successful in the mainstream."*

In this goal we see the common and utterly false belief that including a percentage (typically between 70 and 85) somehow makes a goal measurable. Nothing could be further from the truth. Think about exactly **how** you would **measure** it. What would you **count** to know if Max had been successful in a given class or week or other? If it can't be **objectively assessed**, it isn't measurable! What did the writer mean? Perhaps that Max would pass three of four mainstream classes. If so, that is what should be said: "Max will pass three of the four regular education classes he takes." Or, perhaps the writer meant, "Max would be sent to the office for disciplinary reasons no more than one day in four." If so, that is what should have been said.

*"Sara will make wise choices in her use of leisure time."*

Sara may, indeed, "make wise choices," but we really can't see her doing this. There is no visible learner performance here, nor is there a criterion. Perhaps the writer meant something like: "Sara will attend a supervised, school-sponsored extra-curricular activity at least once a week."

*"Beth will show an appropriate level of upper body strength."*

This goal is easily fixed. The goal writer may well have meant, "Beth will pass the XYZ test of upper body strength at her age level."

*"Anthony will work within a group setting without demonstrating overt behaviors directed at others in the group unless these behaviors are mandated by the group session."*

Surely we don't think this way, do we? Perhaps the truth is that our IEP writer was browsing a computer program's objectives, hoping to find something that might fit Anthony. Better to start with Anthony, as we know him. He bothers other children verbally and physically when they're working. How often does he do this? At least 20–25 times a day. Does this suggest a goal? It should. How about "Anthony will not bother other children inappropriately, verbally or physically, when they are working?" Why 'inappropriately?' Because he might need information or assistance and ask for it very appropriately — a behavior we don't want to discourage. And when we say he will not do it, that is the criterion — zero "bothers."

*"J.B. will use at least two strategies to take responsibility for his anger management with 80% accuracy."*

What in the world did the writer really have in mind? Possibly something like, "J.B. will have no inappropriate displays of anger." Why not say it just like that? The writer might object saying, "I don't expect J.B. to be perfect." OK. How often should J.B. have an inappropriate display of anger by the end of a full year of reteaching? Perhaps all IEP team members agree they would be pleased if he had no more than 1 a month, since he now has 2 or 3 every day. Remember, the goal is saying the IEP team would be pleased with this result by this time.

*"T. will write using various forms to communicate for a variety of purposes and audiences."*

Some goals and their objectives are so totally unmeasurable they deserve little comment. In June, 2004 this goal was prepared in an affluent suburban high school for a student who had a learning disability in written expression: "To write using various forms to communicate for a variety of purposes and audiences."

The four objectives for this totally unmeasurable goal were equally useless:

1. write to reflect on learning,

2. write for problem solving and application,

3. write using forms appropriate to purpose and topic, and

4. write to communicate and report information from research. The same student's goal in reading was "To use strategies within the reading process to construct meaning."

# Vagueness/Specificity

Fairly frequently, a non-measurable, vague and general annual goal will have some objectives or benchmarks which, while not measurable, are far more specific. Alex's IEP illustrates this. Alex is a highly intelligent, 16-year old non-reader who has severe dyslexia and a predictably high level of anger and confusion about why he can't read, write or spell.

The three objectives discussed below appeared on Alex's IEP under the totally non-measurable goal "develop functional academics." To bring order to chaos, we first try to understand what the writer might have intended and then express it in objective, measurable terms. The fact that there is much room for different ideas about what was intended is itself a problem. Let's look at Alex's first objective:

*"Given ten words, Alex shall group letters and pronounce letter sounds in words with 80% accuracy."*

Suppose we were to determine whether Alex has met this progress marker. How do we proceed? Clearly, we give ten words to Alex (perhaps a list) and ask him to do something, but what? Is it possibly as simple as "Alex, would you read these aloud?" That's a good guess, but now there is another problem. Does the list look like "sit, bun, log, cat," or it does it look like "exegesis, ophthalmology, entrepreneur?" Does it make a difference? Of course it does.

What is 80% accuracy in reading the list? If the word "palace" were read as "place" or "tentative" as "tantative" or "when" as "where," what percentage of accuracy do we assign to each effort? Or did the writer really mean that Alex should read 80% of the words accurately? How long a time frame is Alex to be allowed to read the words correctly? One minute, ten minutes, an hour? Perhaps the objective writer meant something like this:

"Given ten unfamiliar, regular CVC words, Alex will decode nine of ten correctly in 20 seconds."

*"Alex will research the history and culture of the given country with 80% accuracy."*

Remembering that Alex apparently reads at a mid-first grade level and is presently working on letter sounds and decoding, what are we to make of this objective? If Alex comes into school tomorrow morning and says, "I researched the history and culture of China without any mistakes last night," are we to check off the objective as completed? Is that what the writer intended? If not, could the objective be rewritten to fit both Alex and the writer's intent? What about something like this:

"Given a one-hour PBS video on the history and culture of China and a tape recorder, after viewing the tape, Alex will dictate and record ten things he learned about China, with no more than one factual error."

*"Through various community service projects Alex will develop a compassionate understanding for those less fortunate and from various cultural/ethnic backgrounds with 80% accuracy."*

The third is even more of a challenge. Where in the world does an objective like this come from? (Perhaps it could be returned.) One thing is clear. Alex is to participate in three or more "various" activities which serve clients who are "less fortunate" and who have cultural/ethnic backgrounds different from Alex's. But how are we to know whether this participation has resulted in "compassionate understanding?"

At some level we all know what compassionate understanding is, but what is acceptable as **evidence** of it would vary widely from one of us to the next. This is one reason there is usually more than one appropriate way to write a given goal or objective.

Ideally, we could look into Alex's heart, soul or mind to see if compassionate understanding is there. Since that is not possible, we must instead ask what behaviors are reasonable, acceptable indicators of compassionate understanding. Here we must remember that Alex is a bright adolescent who is frustrated and confused about why he can't read. This may well be why his teacher selected this arcane objective.

The question is "What behaviors of a 16-year-old could indicate compassionate understanding of the 'less fortunate'?" Clearly, Alex will need guidance and assistance in choosing community service projects in which to get involved. Perhaps Alex's school has a service learning requirement for graduation. One approach to writing a measurable goal here would be to involve the service learning coordinator at Alex's school in his IEP meeting. Once the service learning coordinator understands what we want Alex to accomplish (i.e, compassionate understanding of those less fortunate), the coordinator could suggest several existing community service projects where Alex could interact with individuals who differ from him culturally and economically. How about this for a measurable objective:

"Alex will volunteer with the local Habitat for Humanity organization five hours a week for the next three months. In addition to participating in the current house building project, Alex will interview 3 other volunteers and find out why they chose to be involved in Habitat for Humanity. With the volunteers' permission, Alex will tape record these interviews. Alex will also learn about the family for whom the house is being built, either by talking directly with the family or by interviewing the director of the local Habitat for Humanity project. Alex will either record these interviews or record what he remembers of the interviews as soon as possible afterward. Each month, Alex will meet with his social studies teacher to report on his interviews and share his feelings about the Habitat project."

Admittedly, this is a very complex and lengthy objective. But then, so is developing compassion for others. The purpose of having Alex volunteer with an agency such as Habitat for Humanity is that it provides Alex with a structured situation in which to participate and to observe and learn from other participants who probably already demonstrate "compassion for others" or they would be unlikely to have become involved in such a project. A value such as "compassion" is best learned from others who demonstrate that value in their everyday lives. Having Alex interview and tape the interviews, first with other volunteers, and then with the family who will eventually live in the house Alex is helping to build, will allow Alex to later listen to and reflect on those interviews. Tape recording the interviews means Alex won't have to try to write down the answers to his questions, since his writing skills are probably no stronger than his reading skills. Requiring Alex to meet with his social studies teacher to discuss his volunteer work and his interviews, will give the teacher the opportunity to monitor Alex's participation in the project and ask questions about what Alex is learning from his volunteer ism.

Additional progress markers could be written that designate other community service projects in which Alex will volunteer for 3 months at a time. Alex could complete three such volunteer projects in one school year to meet an annual goal related to providing service to others in the community. Alex would also meet part or all of his service learning requirements for graduation.

The original goal of developing a compassionate understanding with 80% accuracy represents perfectly the absurdity of inserting a percentage with no thought of what it could possibly mean or how it could be assessed.

## Almost Measurable

The above examples of goals have all been quite obviously and blatantly not measurable. However, not all goals have such transparent problems. Some goals appear, at first glance, to be more easily measured than they really are. One good way to check the appropriateness of a GO/B is to imagine the moment of measuring has come. Exactly how will one proceed? Would someone else proceed the same way? These GO/Bs, like the others, are all from real IEPs. They are, however, much closer to measurable.

> *At first glance some goals appear to be more easily measured than they really are. Check carefully and make sure they really are easy to measure.*

*"Steve will participate appropriately in a conversation in four of five opportunities."*

To assess whether Steve can do this, we could stage five situations with peers and adults where Steve would be approached and engaged in conversation. But an element is missing. How well does he have to do this? What if Steve appropriately responds "Hi" to a peer's greeting, but then walks away? Is that sufficient? What if he engages appropriately and he and the conversation partner each offer four appropriate exchanges before Steve suddenly goes on an inappropriate conversational tangent? Is that success?

It is often easy or tempting to think that putting numbers in a goal, such as 4 of 5 trials or with 90% accuracy, automatically make the GO/B measurable. Not so. It takes meaningful quantification, not just random numbers.

*"Terry will read a paragraph and state the main idea with 95% accuracy."*

Think of checking Terry on this goal. What does it mean to state an idea with 95% accuracy? Some people might have a notion of how to do that, but would they all have the same notion? What level of textual material will Terry be reading? Possibly what the writer meant was that if Terry read 100 paragraphs at a 4th–5th grade level, he could correctly state the main idea in at least 95 of them. However, why would the goal be to comprehend less than all of the paragraphs?

*"Given vertical and horizontal straight lines, Natalie will trace them without deviating more than 1" from the line 80% of the time."*

This could be easy for Natalie. If we give her lines less than one inch long, then she can't fail to meet the GO/B, regardless of whether she made any improvement at all. What this writer failed to specify is the length of the lines to be traced. The 80% could be made less ambiguous in this GO/B by simply saying "deviate less than one inch on eight of ten lines, each 6 inches long."

*"J.T. will fill out a timecard with his hours worked each week with 80% accuracy."*

Wouldn't it be better to find a way to enable J.T. to do this with 100% accuracy? Neither the supervisor nor the payroll clerk would be pleased if J.T. performed this GO/B as written. There is no magic in 80% or in any other percent. The goal that "Johnny will cross the street safely 80% of the time" truly makes an important, if humorous, point.

Some districts have actually gone so far as to give their teachers pre-packaged, pre-written GO/Bs, each with one blank for the child's name and another for percentage, e.g., "_____ will do single-digit addition problems with ____% correct." The instruction to the teacher suggests something like "Individualize by inserting 70%, 75% or 80% as appropriate." This preposterous procedure is at best 15% sensible, 1% legal, and 0% best practice! Computer generated progress markers are even less sensible or legal and are even further from best practices.

# Myths of Measurability

While examining these less-than-OK goals, we have encountered several false beliefs that interfere with writing measurable progress markers:

## Myth 1: If a GO/B contains a percentage, it's measurable.

These examples illustrate the myth:

- Luther will control his behavior 80% of the time.

- Eugene will write a paragraph with 75% accuracy.

- Jason will read an expository passage of 500 words and tell the main idea with 90% accuracy 70% of the time.

- Anthony will name 2 ways to control a self-destructive attitude with 75% accuracy.

*Including a percentage does not make a goal measurable.*

## Myth 2: If a GO/B contains technical language or 'words of art,' it must be valid.

These examples illustrate the myth:

- Kevin will improve his central auditory processing.

- Spencer will demonstrate appropriate interpersonal and communication skills.

- Matti will improve visual-motor perceptual skills.

- Kim will internalize values of democracy.

- Gerry will use strategies within the listening process to construct meaning.

- Brandon will be able to answer questions that critically investigate a written passage. (Brandon reads at a beginning second grade level).

- Keenan will explain a procedure concisely, accurately and logically without models or prompts with 90% accuracy.

*Technical language does not make a goal measurable.*

## Myth 3: If a GO/B contains an "action" verb, it is measurable.

These examples illustrate the myth:

- Determine high risk behavior.

- Demonstrate an understanding of dating.

- Demonstrate an understanding of the physical component in emotional and social well-being.

- Ask questions to clarify issues.

- Develop a web to aid passage comprehension.

*An action verb does not guarantee measurability.*

# Questions/Answers

Before we begin applying our knowledge of measurability by writing GO/Bs, it is important to put this knowledge in the broader context of practices that must be followed in preparing IEPs.

On July 1, 2005, when IDEA 2004 amendments take effect, certain important changes must be made to the IEP process. It is crucial that the writing of appropriate goals and progress markers occurs within an overall IEP development process which is consistent with IDEA and with best practice.[3] Among the IDEA 2004 changes that affect IEPs are these[4]:

1. Short-term objectives or benchmarks are required only on the IEPs of those students who are assessed by alternate assessments using alternate (not grade-level) achievement standards; however, all IEPs must contain "a description of how the childs' progress toward meeting the annuals will be measured and when periodic reports on the progress" will be provided;

2. The special education, related services and supplementary aids and services written into the IEP must be "based on peer-reviewed research to the extent practicable";

3. A member of the IEP team may be excused from attendance at an IEP meeting if the parents and school district agree, and additionally, if that person's area of the curriculum is to be discussed, prior written input is provided to the parent and the rest of the team;

4. Transition services are included on the IEP when the student becomes 16[5] years of age;

5. At each annual IEP meeting parents and the district may agree to make any changes by written documents rather than further meetings.

Our ideas about IEPs, IEP meetings, and goals are formed largely from our own experiences and are often limited to how one school district or building staff handle these matters. The bigger picture comes from IDEA itself and most especially from

---

3. See, e.g., Herr, C. and Bateman, D. 2005, **Better IEP Meetings**. Verona, WI.
4. All quotes are directly from IDEA 2004.
5. Prior to July 1, 2005 IEPs were required to address transition needs for 14-year-olds.

two appendices to the IDEA regulations. The first of these, called Appendix C, was published in 1981. The second, Appendix A, accompanied the 1999 IDEA regulations. Together the two answer 100 of the most common questions about IEPs. We have selected a few from each appendix, chosen because they provide legal guidance on important and frequently misunderstood matters related to IEPs, the IDEA process and goals.

# From Appendix C (1981):

*Must related services personnel attend IEP meetings?*

**No. It is not required that they attend.** However, if a handicapped child has an identified need for related services, it would be appropriate for the related services personnel to attend the meeting or otherwise be involved in developing the IEP. For example, when the child's evaluation indicates the need for a specific related service (e.g., physical therapy, occupational therapy or counseling), the agency should ensure that a qualified provider of that service either (1) attends the IEP meeting, or (2) provides a written recommendation concerning the nature, frequency, and amount of service to be provided to the child. (Question #23)

*(Editor's note: The highlighting is for emphasis and does not appear in the original text.)*

*What should be included in the statement of the child's present levels of educational performance?*

The statement of present levels of educational performance will be different for each handicapped child. Thus, determinations about the content of the statement for an individual child are matters that are left to the discretion of participants in the IEP meetings. However, the following are some points which should be taken into account in writing this part of the IEP.

1. The statement should accurately describe the effect of the child's handicap on the child's performance in any area of education that is affected, including (1) academic areas ( reading, math, communication, etc.), and (2) non-academic areas (daily life activities, mobility, etc.).

2. The statement should be written in objective measurable terms, to the extent possible. Data from the child's evaluation would be a good source of such information. Test scores that are pertinent to the child's diagnosis might be included, where appropriate. However, the scores should be (1) self-explanatory (i.e., they can be interpreted by all participants without the use of test manuals or other aids), or (2) an explanation should be included. Whatever test results are used should reflect the impact of the handicap on the child's performance. Thus, raw scores would not usually be sufficient.

3. **There should be a direct relationship between the present levels of educational performance and the other components of the IEP. Thus, if the statement describes a problem with the child's reading level and points to a deficiency in a specific reading skill, this problem should be addressed under both (1) goals and objectives, and (2) specific special education and related services to be provided to the child.** (Question #36) **[emphasis added]**

*Should there be a relationship between the goals and objectives in the IEP and those that are in instructional plans of special education personnel?*

Yes. There should be a direct relationship between the IEP goals and objectives for a given handicapped student and the goals and objectives that are in the special education instructional plans for the child. However, the IEP is not intended to be detailed enough to be used as an instructional plan. The IEP, through its goals and objectives, (1) sets the general direction to be taken by those who will implement the IEP, and (2) serves as the basis for developing a detailed instructional plan for the child. (Question #41)

*Does the IEP include only special education and related services or does it describe the total education of the child?*

The IEP is required to include **only those matters concerning the provision of special education and related services and the extent to which the child can participate in regular education programs.** (NOTE: The regulations define "special education" as specially designed instruction to meet the unique needs of a handicapped child, and "related services" as those which are necessary to assist the child to benefit from special education.) (See Secs. 300.14 and 300.13 respectively.)

For some handicapped children, the IEP will only address a very limited part of their education (e.g., for a speech impaired child, the IEP would generally be limited to the child's speech impairment). For other children (e.g., those who are profoundly retarded), the IEP might cover their total education. An IEP for a child with a physical impairment but no mental impairment might consist only of specially designed physical education. However, if the child also has a mental impairment, the IEP might cover most of the child's education. (Question #47)

# From Appendix A (1999):

*Must the measurable annual goals in a child's IEP address all areas of the general curriculum, or only those areas in which the child's involvement and progress are affected by the child's disability?*

Section 300.347 (a) (2) requires that each child's IEP include "A statement of measurable annual goals, including benchmarks or short-term objectives, related to- (i) *meeting the child's needs that result from the child's disability to enable the child to be involved in and progress in the general curriculum* . . . ; and (ii) meeting each of the child's other educational needs that result from the child's disability . . ."

Thus, a public agency is **not** required to include in an IEP annual goals that relate to areas of the general curriculum in which the child's disability does not affect the child's ability to be involved in and progress in the general curriculum. If a child with a disability needs only modifications or accommodations in order to progress in an area of the general curriculum, the IEP does not need to include a goal for that area; however, the IEP would need to specify those modifications or accommodations.

Public agencies often require all children, including children with disabilities, to demonstrate mastery in a given area of the general curriculum before allowing them to progress to the next level or grade in that area. Thus, in order to ensure that each child with a disability can effectively demonstrate competencies in an applicable area of the general curriculum, it is important for the IEP team to consider the accommodations and modifications that the child needs to assist him or her in demonstrating progress in that area. (Question #4)

*What is a public agency's responsibility if it is not possible to reach consensus on what services should be included in a child's IEP?*

The IEP meeting serves as a communication vehicle between parents and school personnel, and enables them, as equal participants, to make joint, informed decisions regarding the (1) child's needs and appropriate goals; (2) extent to which the child will be involved in the general curriculum and participate in the regular education environment and State and district-wide assessments; and (3) services needed to support that involvement and participation and to achieve agreed-upon goals. Parents are considered equal partners with school personnel in making these decisions, and the IEP team must consider the parents' concerns and the information that they provide regarding their child in developing, reviewing, and revising IEPs (§§§§300.343 (c) (iii) and 300.346 (a) (1) and (b)).

The IEP team should work toward consensus, but the public agency has ultimate responsibility to ensure that the IEP includes the services that the child needs in order to receive FAPE. It is not appropriate to make IEP decisions based upon a majority "vote." If the team cannot reach consensus, the public agency must provide the parents with prior written notice of the agency's proposals or refusals, or both, regarding the child's educational program, and the parents have the right to seek resolution of any disagreements by initiating an impartial due process hearing.

Every effort should be made to resolve differences between parents and school staff through voluntary mediation or some other informal step, without resort to a due process hearing. However, mediation or other informal procedures may not be used to deny or delay a parent's right to a due process hearing, or to deny any other rights afforded under Part B. (Question #9)

*Who can serve as the representative of the public agency at an IEP meeting?*

The IEP team must include a representative of the public agency who: (a) is qualified to provide, or supervise the provision of, specially designed instruction to meet the unique needs of children with disabilities; (b) is knowledgeable about the general curriculum; and (c) is knowledgeable about the availability of resources of the public agency (§§300.344 (a) (4)).

Each public agency may determine which specific staff member will serve as the agency representative in a particular IEP meeting, so long as the individual meets these requirements. It is important, however, that the agency representative have the authority to commit agency resources and be able to ensure that whatever services are set out in the IEP will actually be provided.

A public agency may designate another public agency member of the IEP team to also serve as the agency representative, so long as that individual meets the requirements of §§300.344 (a) (4). (Question #22)

*What is the role of a regular education teacher in the development, review and revision of the IEP for a child who is, or may be, participating in the regular education environment?*

As required by §§300.344 (a) (2), the IEP team for a child with a disability must include at least one regular education teacher of the child if the child is, or may be, participating in the regular education environment. Section 300.346 (d) further specifies that the regular education teacher of a child with a disability, as a member of the IEP team, must, to the extent appropriate[6], participate in the development,

---

6. IDEA 2004 allows a team member to be excused from attendance at an IEP meeting if the district and parents agree so in writing. If the excused member's area of knowledge is to be discussed at the meeting, that member must provide written input to the district and parent prior to the meeting.

review, and revision of the child's IEP, including assisting in (1) the determination of appropriate positive behavioral interventions and strategies for the child; and (2) the determination of supplementary aids and services, program modifications, and supports for school personnel that will be provided for the child, consistent with 300.347 (a) (3) (§§300.344(d)).

Thus, while a regular education teacher must be a member of the IEP team if the child is, or may be, participating in the regular education environment, the teacher need not (depending upon the child's needs and the purpose of the specific IEP team meeting) be required to participate in all decisions made as part of the meeting or to be present throughout the entire meeting or attend every meeting. For example, the regular education teacher who is a member of the IEP team must participate in discussions and decisions about how to modify the general curriculum in the regular classroom to ensure the child's involvement and progress in the general curriculum and participation in the regular education environment.

Depending upon the specific circumstances, however, it may not be necessary for the regular education teacher to participate in discussions and decisions regarding, for example, the physical therapy needs of the child, if the teacher is not responsible for implementing that portion of the child's IEP.

In determining the extent of the regular education teacher's participation at IEP meetings, public agencies and parents should discuss and try to reach agreement on whether the child's regular education teacher that is a member of the IEP team should be present at a particular IEP meeting and, if so, for what period of time. The extent to which it would be appropriate for the regular education teacher member of the IEP team to participate in IEP meetings must be decided on a case-by-case basis. (Question #24)

*Is it permissible for an agency to have the IEP completed before the IEP meeting begins?*

**No**. Agency staff may come to an IEP meeting prepared with evaluation findings and proposed recommendations regarding IEP content, but the agency must make it clear to the parents at the outset of the meeting that the services proposed by the agency are only recommendations for review and discussion with the parents. Parents have the right to bring questions, concerns, and recommendations to an IEP meeting as part of a full discussion, of the child's needs and the services to be provided to meet those needs before the IEP is finalized.

Public agencies must ensure that, if agency personnel bring drafts of some or all of the IEP content to the IEP meeting, there is a full discussion with the child's parents, before the child's IEP is finalized, regarding drafted content and the child's needs and the services to be provided to meet those needs. (Question #32)

———————————

Another important question frequently asked in the real world after people have learned the simple efficient process described in this book is, "How do I fit this way of writing GO/Bs onto the IEP form I'm required to use?" We will return to this question after "this way" has been presented, but it may be helpful to be aware of the need to deal with it.

# Part II: Writing Goals and Objectives

# Introduction

As we launch into writing GO/Bs, it is reassuring to first recall that no teacher is liable for a child's failure to reach a GO/B when:

1. The goal is reasonable in light of what was (or should have been) known about the student, her or his PLOP and the effectiveness of the service to be provided; and

2. A good-faith effort was made to help the student accomplish the goal.
   A "good-faith" effort means that:

   a. Each progress marker was measurable and measured at the appropriate report period; and

   b. If and when it became evident that a progress marker would not be reached at the present rate of achievement, something was changed immediately, e.g., the intensity of the service was increased, a different methodology was employed, or further task analysis or perhaps diagnostic assessment was undertaken.

A useful process for writing goals and objectives makes the measuring and reporting of student progress as simple, efficient and economical as possible. And consistent with that simplicity and efficiency, recall that **goals**, **objectives**, **benchmarks** and **progress markers** are **exactly the same** except for the amount of time required to reach an annual goal.

*Goals, objectives, benchmarks and progress markers are the same things.*

Annual goals are required by IDEA, and they are simply the objectives or benchmarks to be reached in 12 months. Short-term objectives or benchmarks are also required by IDEA[7], and progress toward them must be reported to parents at least as often as every reporting (grading) period for non-disabled children. Almost all school districts in the nation use either a 9-week or a 6-week reporting period. For a 9-week

---

7. As said earlier, short-term objectives or benchmarks are still required for those students who, under No Child Left Behind, are assessed against alternate rather than grade-level standards. Those students constitute roughly 10% of the students who have IEPs.

reporting schedule, there will be a minimum of three objectives (1st nine weeks), (2nd nine weeks), (3rd nine weeks) and the annual goal (4th and last nine weeks). For a 6-week schedule, there would be at least five objectives and the goal.

The present levels of performance (PLOPs) are the starting point in the goal/progress marker development process. These PLOPs are linked to the annual goal by the progress markers. The third element is the service to be provided to move the child's performance from the present level to the accomplishment of the goal. The IEP team, parents and professionals together, should never lose focus on what the child needs (stated as a PLOP), how the child's need will be addressed (service) and what the child will accomplish (GO/Bs) as a result of the services.

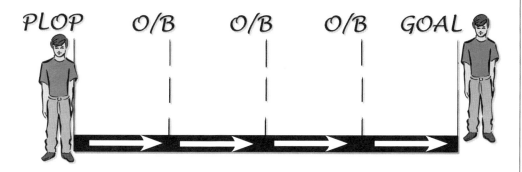

# GO/Bs in Perspective

The fundamental purpose of the IEP is to specify the unique educational needs of the student, the services the school district will provide to address those needs and the expected results of the services.

In some districts IEP team members are allowed, encouraged or even required to use either the child's placement or the curriculum, rather than the child's needs, as the starting point for the IEP. This practice is a blatant and serious violation of IDEA. If the IEPs for all the resource room language arts students are highly similar, it shows that the ongoing resource room program, rather than the students' needs, was driving the IEP content. Another version of the wrong starting place is the "standards" or general curriculum-driven approach where the team tries to write an appropriate goal for the student in each major curriculum area. This erroneous practice comes from failing to recognize that the IEP is to address skills necessary for the student to access the general curriculum, such as following directions, completing assignments independently, working cooperatively in small groups or reading grade level material. The general curriculum itself need not appear routinely in IEPs. We should remind ourselves as often as necessary that the IEP is a special education document and that the "I" stands for Individualized.

The unique needs of the child are those that are to be addressed by special education or other special services. The IEP is a **special education document**, and the goals should be limited to special education and to that which is individualized within the child's total education program. After all, an IEP is an "individualized" education program, is it not? And what is special education? It is legally defined as "**specially designed instruction** to meet the unique needs of the child." Specially designed instruction includes **adapted content**, **methodology**, and **delivery of service**.

*The first step in writing measurable goals is to list the child's needs, in plain, everyday language.*

Every significant need of the student that requires adapted content (i.e., modified or different curriculum), adapted methodology (e.g., sign language or multi-sensory, synthetic phonics) or adapted delivery of services (e.g.,

1:1 teaching or a minimally distracting environment) should be identified by the IEP team and addressed by the IEP. Needs will be of two types — (1) what the child needs to learn to do, or to do better, and (2) conditions the child needs (requires) in order to learn efficiently and effectively. The first requires a **present level of performance** from which the learning can be measured by the GO/Bs. The second, the conditions the child needs, e.g., 1:1 teaching, a highly structured class, a quiet environment, are just as important. They do not require a PLOP, and instead are to be addressed in the mandated **statement of services** to be provided or sometimes under Modifications and Accommodations.

# The Writing Process

Conceptually, the process of writing appropriate, measurable goals and progress markers begins with getting a clear picture of the child's unique needs. This is done in two ways — by examining all the assessment information about the student for performance deficits or weaknesses, and by asking parents, teachers and others who know the student well.

One question that can be very helpful in identifying areas of need is "What three or four things that she doesn't do now would we most like for Patricia to be able **to do** or **to do better** by the end of the year?" Similarly, there are times when we also ask, "What three or four things that Jeff does now would we like for him **not to do** by the end of the year?"

> *When the student needs to learn TO DO or TO DO BETTER, a present level of performance must be stated.*

In preparation for the IEP meeting, when the team will identify and agree upon the student's needs, both parents and teachers can take some initial steps. Imagine that the IEP meeting has been scheduled and you've been asked to give some thought ahead of time to developing measurable goals and objectives for Corey. When you ask, "What would I like for Corey to be able to do by the end of the year?" thoughts come tumbling out . . .

I'd like Corey to:

• put on his own coat, take it off, and hang it up,

• share toys and materials without crying or hitting,

• speak in longer phrases or sentences,

• learn to count by rote to 100 and count objects to 10,

• print his name without a model and copy the alphabet legibly,

• color within the lines and cut on the lines,

• use a larger vocabulary.

These first ideas are specific and in perfectly ordinary, everyday language. They need to stay that way! Specific and plain. The last thing that should be done is to fancy them up. The first example above could be stated "to improve level of independence in self-help," while the second could become "transition from parallel to interactive, cooperative play with peers." These would be steps in exactly the wrong direction. One doesn't have to ask what is meant by taking off a coat or sharing toys. The clearer the language, the better.

If the next step is not to convert the language into counterproductive jargon, what is it? It may be to think about whether a desired performance is a full year goal itself, or part of a larger group of tasks to be taught. "Use a larger vocabulary" can well be worked on all year, while "putting on and removing a coat and hanging it up" could be part of a larger cluster of skills including shoe tying, buttoning, coloring and cutting and more that would comprise an annual goal.

Another bit of preparation is to give thought to prioritizing goals for the next year. If a goal is met early, another can be added, if appropriate. While there is no legal guideline, experience shows that approximately 2–5 goals can address many children's most important unique needs. Now suppose the IEP team has met and agreed upon this list of Jamie's most important needs:

- better self-control,

- more legible handwriting,

- to read better,

- a highly structured classroom,

- direct instruction and frequent review,

- access to a 'cool down' area.

If the IEP team is aware of other needs and goals which they have decided to postpone until a later time, make a note of that to guard against a claim that needs were ignored or undetected.

The individual, unique needs that are agreed upon must be dealt with on the IEP. However, not all of a child's unique needs must be treated similarly. As we said earlier, some needs require a goal and, therefore, a present level of performance. Others do not need a PLOP. Jamie's first three needs are "to learn to do or do better"; therefore, each requires a PLOP.

| Jamie's Needs | Jamie's PLOP |
|---|---|
| Better self-control | Averages 2–5 inappropriate outbursts daily |
| Legible handwriting (or printing) | Copies 12 letters legibly per minute |
| Functional reading skills | A sight vocabulary of 14 words; no decoding skills |

*When the need is for a service or accommodation (e.g., frequent review or a highly structured class), no PLOP is required, but the service MUST be on the IEP.*

If the need is for a particular condition or accommodation, it does not require a PLOP. It is to be included on the IEP in the required "statement of special education" or perhaps in the Modifications and Accommodations section. Where on the IEP the need is addressed is not important. What is essential is that it is addressed.

| Jamie's Needs | Condition (No PLOP required) |
|---|---|
| Highly structured class | Highly structured class |
| Direct instruction | Direct instruction |
| Access to a "cool down" area | A 'cool down' area |

After all the major needs of the student have been identified and perhaps prioritized, the next step, as shown above, is to determine which require a stated, objective, measurable PLOP.

# Present Levels of Performance (PLOPs)

Most IEP forms contain a section called "Present Levels of Performance" or "Educational Status." Typically this is completed by a lengthy narrative about the student, often including information on the family, the disability, school history and more, plus all the assessment data from speech and language evaluations, psychological and psychoeducational evaluations and more.

*Present levels of performance must be measured, current, and accurate.*

At least three major problems can be seen in this practice. First, it is a colossal and unnecessary waste of time to copy information from one document to another, e.g., from evaluation reports to the IEP. Second, the information is almost always one to three years outdated and lacks the precision and currency essential for its most important purpose, i.e., as the **starting point from which the year's progress is to be measured**. If one wants to know how much weight Joe lost (i.e., how much progress has been made), one obviously must know Joe's beginning weight. To know whether Jezebel's attendance has improved, we must know what it was before. How one performs now — i.e., what the starting point is — is crucial in setting an appropriate goal for any given period of time. Whether the house under construction can be completed by next Friday depends on how far along it is today. Whether reading 8th grade material at a rate of 150 wpm with only random error is a reasonable annual goal depends on that student's present reading level, as well as on his or her intellectual ability, and most of all on the quality and intensity of the instruction.

In the previous section we moved from three of Jamie's needs to "starting point" PLOPs. The first need was for "better self-control" and the PLOP was that Jamie presently averages 2-5 inappropriate outbursts daily. The key fact here is that we have a point from which we can determine whether Jamie is making progress. If we just knew that Jamie needs better self-control (or anger management), we would be hard-pressed to say whether 1-3 outbursts daily was progression, regression or no change. We must have an actual measured point, a PLOP, from which progress can be evaluated.

Jamie's second PLOP was "copies 12 letters legibly per minute." Again, without that information, we'd have no way to know whether his next-month rate of 20 letters per minute is an improvement. The last PLOP for Jamie — a 14 sight word vocabulary and no decoding skills — provides a starting point for measurement, and a direction for instruction, i.e., teach decoding from the beginning.

Once we have a specific, measured PLOP, we can begin to write an appropriate goal and its progress markers. When we say "measured," we recognize that many perfectly useful PLOPs are based on best remembered "guesstimates," such as how frequently Johnny hits other children ("at least 3 times every day, sometimes as many as 6 or 7"). The point is that we have a known starting level from which progress can be measured. An observation that he **never** hangs up his coat is a perfectly useful beginning level.

# Writing Goals and Objectives/Benchmarks/Progress Markers

As we begin the actual process of writing PLOPs and GO/Bs, we look to ladders and pies. First, however, is the Grand Rule of GO/Bs — there is more than one right way to write any measurable goal or objective. For almost every example of a good GO/B, there are additional appropriate ways it could have been written. The vital element in a GO/B is always **objective measurability**. Each reader will think of other ways objectives or goals could have been stated. As long as they're **measurable**, they're fine!

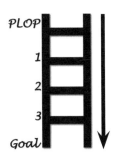

*Fig. 2a*

## Ladders

Goals and their progress markers come in two styles — "ladders" and "pies." First, ladders: The bottom (or top) rung in the ladder is the PLOP and the top (or bottom) rung is the annual goal. The in-between rungs are the objectives or benchmarks, one for each grading/reporting period. The annual goal is simply the progress marker for the last grading/reporting period. All the rungs, including the PLOP and the annual goal, use the same unit of measurement.

Some of us are more comfortable thinking and writing from 'up' to 'down' (see Fig. 2a). Others like the idea of building 'up' (see Fig. 2b). Either way works.

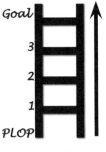

*Fig. 2b*

Perhaps building 'up' (Fig. 2b) works best conceptually, but climbing down the ladder (Fig. 2a) may be a more familiar, comfortable progression. We'll use climbing down from PLOP to goal (safe on the ground).

*The PLOP, objectives/benchmarks/progress markers and goal must all be in the same units of measurement.*

For ladder-type GO/Bs, all the rungs from PLOP to annual goal must use the **same units of measurement**. Below are examples of abbreviated and "lying-on-their-side" ladders. These have only one progress marker instead of the usual three or more, to illustrate the necessity of keeping the same units of measurement throughout the sequence.

| PLOP | Illustrative Progress Marker | Annual Goal |
|---|---|---|
| a. Unexcused absences and tardies average 5 a week. | Unexcused absences and tardies average 2 a week. | Unexcused absences and tardies average less than one a week. |
| b. Orally reads 3rd grade text at 25 wpm with 5-10 errors. | Orally reads 3rd grade text at 50 wpm with 0-2 errors. | Orally reads 3rd grade text at 90 wpm with 0-2 errors. |
| c. Spells 30 words dictated from 7th grade list with 50% correct. | Spells 30 words dictated from 7th grade list with 75% correct. | Spells 30 words dictated from 7th grade list with 95% correct. |
| d. Given a page of 20 clock faces, writes correct time at a rate of 6 per minute with 2-3 errors. | Given a page of 20 clock faces, writes correct time at a rate of 15 per minute with no more than 1 error. | Given a page of 20 clock faces, writes correct time at a rate of 20 per minute with 0 errors. |
| e. Tantrums an average of 50 minutes per week. | Tantrums an average of less than 5 minutes per week. | Tantrums an average of 0/zero minutes per week. |
| f. When approached by a peer, J. always runs away. | When approached by a peer, J. runs away less than half the time. | When approached by a peer, J. never runs away. |
| g. On the XYZ Reading Test[8], scores 2.9 grade level.[9] | On the XYZ Reading Test, scores 3.5 grade level. | On the XYZ Reading Test, scores 4.3 grade level. |
| h. Instantly and correctly recognizes 20 of the ABC Sight Words List. | Instantly and correctly recognizes 90 of the ABC Sight Words List. | Instantly and correctly recognizes 120 of the ABC Sight Words List. |
| i. Independently walks about 4 steps before falling. | Independently walks across the room without falling. | Independently walks on even surfaces without falling. |
| j. Assists in dressing self by pulling pants up and shirt down. | Assists in dressing self by putting on underwear, t-shirt, and pants. | Dresses self except for buttoning and shoe tying. |

---

8. Read "XYZ" as your favorite standardized reading test.

9. The use of grade level is not desirable for many reasons, including its lack of reliability, the inappropriateness of repeated administrations of the same test combined with lack of comparability of a different test, and the extreme inefficiency of using so much time on testing.

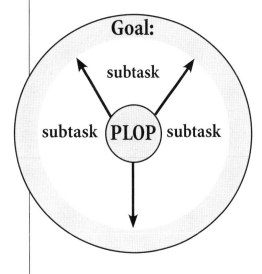

## Pies

Pies are different from ladders in that in a pie the order of completing each piece or subpart of the learning task is unimportant. Sometimes all the pieces or parts of the task may be worked on simultaneously. The order of completion matters little or not at all. Progress in each subtask may be assessed separately and in different units. In the following example, Bethany will have reached the goal (outer rim of the pie), when all three subtasks are mastered.

## Pie example #1

**PLOP:** Bethany looks down at the ground when an individual starts talking to her, moves 2 or more feet away and doesn't respond when the person introduces himself/herself.

**GOAL:** Bethany will stay or move to within one foot of a person who initiates verbal interaction, will maintain eye contact as long as that person is talking to her, and will respond to introductions by looking the person in the eye and saying, "Hi, my name is Bethany."

- Bethany will stay or move to within one foot of a person who initiates a verbal interaction with her.

- Bethany will maintain eye contact with another individual as long as that person is talking to her.

**Subtasks**

- When someone introduces himself/herself to Bethany by saying, "Hi, my name is _____," Bethany will look the person in the eye and respond by saying, "Hi, my name is Bethany."

## Pie example #2

A second pie example is learning to tell time. Unless one uses only digital time pieces, learning to tell time requires that the student be able to (a) count to 60, at least by 5s, (b) show which direction the hands move (to know whether a hand has not reached or has passed a numeral), (c) identify the numerals or their substitutes (e.g., dots on a watch face), and (d) apply the rule that "the little hand points (to the hour) and the big hand counts (the minutes)." All of these pie pieces need to be mastered but the order matters little. If all slices

**Goal: Tell time to nearest 5 minutes**

PLOP does not tell time

Subtask: Show which directions the hands move and apply the rule "if it isn't there yet, it isn't there"

Subtask: Count to 60 by 5s

Subtask: Apply the rule that the little hand points (to the hour) and the big one counts (the minutes)

Subtask: Identify numerals 1-12 or their substitutes

of a pie are worked on together, it's possible that none would be mastered by the end of a grading period. Special care is then required to report progress accurately and meaningfully.

So far we have glossed over the difference, if any, between objectives and benchmarks. According to IDEA, short-term objectives "break the skills described in the annual goal down into discrete components," while benchmarks describe "the amount of progress the child is expected to make within specified segments of the year" (Appendix A, Question 1). Thus, technically speaking, the subtasks in a pie are objectives and our ladder rungs are benchmarks which specify the amount of progress anticipated each grading period. However the distinction seems to make very little difference and the term "progress markers" includes both.

# A Quick Review — PLOPs

In writing measurable goals and objectives, the first step is to **identify the child's unique needs**. Next, for the major needs that require a goal (i.e., it is something the student **needs to learn to do**), the **PLOP must be specific**, **objective**, and **measurable**. The PLOP must be current, accurate and specific because it is the point from which future progress will be measured. The unit in which it is measured will be the measurable unit for the goal and the progress markers.

Once we have the PLOP, we can begin to write the GO/B. To be measurable, a goal or progress marker must contain an **observable learner performance**, specify the **criterion or level** of satisfactory performance and include any essential **givens or conditions**. For example, *Given* a 10 second-long, tape recorded song of each of 50 North American birds, Jay will promptly and correctly *name* 48 of the 50 birds.

# Writing Measurable GO/Bs

The moment has come to put it all together. Let us suppose that the IEP meeting reveals that before Danny can be successful in the general curriculum in a regular class, he must learn to raise his hand and wait until he is called on rather than loudly blurting out whatever is on his mind at any time.

Will it take a whole year to teach him this? Probably not. Nevertheless, this behavior is important to the regular teacher on the IEP team and it will become a goal. Perhaps it can be reached in a few weeks and then replaced by a different goal. The teacher tells us Danny currently has 20-30 "blurts" a day and no hand raises. We now have a current and accurate PLOP.

But another question presents itself. Is it better to state our goal in terms of decreasing blurts or increasing hand raises? Or both? The blurts are the problem according to the concerned teacher. Of course, the overall plan will be to replace blurts with hand raises, so both are involved. We can track both. Since our initial "service" will include ignoring blurts and positively reinforcing hand raises, tracking both seems reasonable.

Sometimes it is easier or more efficient to think first of writing the annual goal. Other times, it might work better to begin with writing the first progress marker and move toward the goal. Here it seems very clear that we want Danny to have zero blurts. Most children have no blurts. There is no reason Danny has to blurt. The goal is straightforward:  Danny will have zero blurt-outs.

Now, how quickly do we expect how much progress? Recall that Danny's PLOP is 20-30 blurts a day. Let's assume we come up with an effective intervention (service) such as a potent reinforcer for every hand raise with no blurt. If our plan is working, shouldn't we see a fairly rapid drop in blurts? Sometimes we project more than "proportional" or "even rate" progress. If we are on the right track, perhaps we can project that by the end of the first grading period, Danny will have almost no blurts and then the remainder of the grading period our progress markers can be focused on maintaining a near-zero rate.

Having thought aloud, let's see where we are:

**PLOP:**  Danny has 20-30 blurt-outs a day. We want him to raise his hand instead.

**Obj. 1:**  Danny will raise his hand 7 out of 10 times when he wants to say something.

**Obj. 2:**  Danny will raise his hand 8 out of 10 times.

**Obj. 3:**  Danny will raise his hand 9 out of 10 times.

**Annual Goal:**  Danny will always raise his hand.

Is it really that simple? Yes, it can be. Once we have a measured PLOP and a reasonable, measurable goal in the same units (in Danny's case the unit was **number of hand raises**), we use our best judgment, write reasonable progress markers, and specify the service needed.

# A Quick Review — Goals

First, we must have a specific, measured PLOP. Next, we ask what is a reasonable annual goal? Then we examine how much progress per grading period seems to make sense. There are no magical or mathematical formulas. We use the best combination of experience, professional judgment, common sense and goodwill among the team members. To quibble over projections of how much progress is reasonable in each grading period is preposterous. If our projection is found to be wrong (at the end of a grading period), we adjust accordingly.

# Factors in Projecting the Annual Goal

Courts unanimously agree that in judging whether a child's progress has been sufficient, we must make an **individualized determination, taking into account the child's intellectual ability**. Other things being equal, we would obviously project greater gains for a gifted student than for one who has mental retardation. In a case that eventually went to the U.S. Supreme Court, the school personnel were chastised for setting goals of only 4 months gain per year in both reading and math when the student involved had average or above average intelligence.[10] This kind of goal setting error occurs when goals are based solely on past rate of progress.

> *. . . in judging whether a child's progress has been sufficient, we must make an individualized determination, taking into account the child's intellectual ability.*

A closely related error is that of wrongly using a disability as the reason for low goal setting. For instance, some say "Joe has a learning disability in math. Therefore, we should project an annual goal of only a few months in math," even though Joe may have above average intelligence. Or, "Jose has dyslexia, so he will make only a half year of progress in reading during the coming year." It is better to assume we will find

---

10. *Florence Co. Sch.Dist. Four v. Carter*, 510 U.S. 7 (1993)

and use the appropriate methodologies that will be effective for Joe and Jose and will enable them to make more rapid progress. The IEP team is more likely to be faulted for projecting insufficient progress than for being overly optimistic.

Another factor that can enter into goal setting is what is known about the effectiveness of the teacher and the program to be used. For example, daily 1:1 Orton-Gillingham tutoring or small group Direct Instruction with a qualified, experienced teacher would be expected to provide far greater gains than would result from a resource room placement for 45 minutes three times a week with 18 other students and a new teacher not certified in special education or remedial reading.

Another factor in goal setting is the importance we attach to the goal and the quality of focus on it. Suppose that Kassie is a 5th grader struggling to read between 2nd and 3rd grade material. Next year she will enter middle school where she'll be lost if she cannot read independently. We need to make a real push this year to get her to a solid fourth or even fifth grade level. We are willing to sacrifice something else to get her to an independent level in reading, and we believe it can be done. With the IEP team's agreement, Kassie's approval, and everyone's recognition of the importance of reading, we set a goal for the year: "Given 5th grade reading material, Kassie will read orally at 120 cwpm and will correctly answer 9 of 10 literal comprehension questions over that material." It's a high expectation which all parties support. The service, in turn, must be geared to producing this desired outcome.

Jim, on the other hand, is 17 years old and has moderate mental retardation. Over the last ten years he has gradually achieved a sight vocabulary of a few functional words such as "men," "women," "caution," "poison." The IEP team believes that other abilities such as simple meal preparation and job skills are at least as important for him now as reading. We might select a modest goal of a dozen additional functional sight words.

In sum, goal setting is based on experience, common sense, team input and professional judgment. It takes into account the abilities of the student and the importance of the goal area to the student at the time.

# Moving the Child's Performance from PLOP to Goal

IDEA 2004 requires that every IEP include a statement of the special education and related services and supplementary aids and services based on peer-reviewed research to the extent practicable, to be provided to the child ... (and) ... the program modifications or supports for school personnel that will be provided for the child ... (20 USC §1414).

Even though this book is about goals, the services to enable the child to reach his or her goals are so important they can't be ignored.

Common practice on IEPs is to write "special education" in one box and "299 minutes a week" in an adjoining box, "speech therapy" next to "20 min. a week," and so on. Arguably, that practice does not fulfill the intent of the requirement for a "statement." Regardless of its legal sufficiency, this practice is not educationally helpful, nor does it communicate well to parents. Some even believe that "1730 minutes a quarter" of a service is intended to be difficult to grasp.

What is a parent to understand about the actual services being delivered to the child when all the IEP says is 2 hours of special education daily? Does that mean 1:1, small group, resource room with 20 students present, a combination or none of the above? Is it with an aide, a regular education teacher, a special education teacher, an "emergency" certified teacher or other? Is it discovery-based learning, direct instruction, cooperative learning or other? The range of teaching activities subsumed under "special education" is nearly unlimited. It is safe to say that many parents would be shocked to see the service their child is actually receiving in contrast to their perhaps naive belief about the service being provided.

Specificity in describing the services to be provided is as desirable as it is in writing goals and progress markers. For this reason some of the examples provided later include a specification of the service planned to address each particular goal.

# Putting the PLOP — Progress Markers — Goal Sequences on the Form

As was mentioned earlier, many IEP forms have an initial, large space (page or more) for the student's Present Levels of Performance (PLOPs). These PLOPs are often outdated and imbedded in a lengthy narrative. Once in a while this portion of the IEP becomes contentious because parents see it as a "portrait" of their child and want it to show the child in the most positive light possible. Often they want it to have far more and different detail than IDEA requires. Having the PLOP section of the IEP lengthy, far-ranging and physically removed from the GO/Bs makes it difficult, but not impossible, to focus on a PLOP as the one essential beginning point for its corresponding GO/B.

Once a handful of goal areas has been selected, we should pull from the PLOP section any pertinent data that may be there. Frequently there won't be much because the evaluation data is often far more global, general and old than is useful for a goal starting point. To illustrate the problem, let's use the common area of reading. Suppose our student is a 6th grader (end of year) and the PLOP (actually measured one full year ago when he had his 3-year re-evaluation) says the XYZ (or W-J III, etc.) Reading Test scores were: Broad reading — 3.1 grade level, Comprehension — 3.4 grade level, and Word Reading — 2.7 grade level. The first problem is that the scores are a full year old. Second, which of the 3 scores should we use? Third, how are we going to report progress every grading period? Surely no one would propose giving the same, lengthy, individual standardized reading test four times in one year . . . or would one?

Now compare that to the useful information the teacher obtained for the IEP team yesterday when he had Jake read aloud from his instructional level text material for 3 one-minute periods. The teacher learned that Jake reads 3rd grade material at 80-100 correct words per minute (cwpm). That is a PLOP we can work with! Some IEP forms now have a page for each goal and its objectives. However, if there isn't space on the goal page designated for the PLOP for that goal, jot the PLOP at the top or bottom of the page or in the margin as close as possible to the progress marker for the first grading period. A few IEP forms have also not yet linked the progress markers to grading periods. If yours has not, just number them to correspond to the end of each grading period, with the goal as the final period.

A useful, simple and legally correct form will, (1) display the **sequence** from the PLOP thru progress markers to GOAL, (2) link each progress marker and goal to the actual measurement and reporting of it, and (3) show the **service** to be provided to allow accomplishment of the goal.

Two such sample forms are shown here. Each of the samples in the next section, as well as any other measurable PLOP — progress marker — GOAL sequences can readily be shown on either of these forms.

*Form 1*

# PLOP — Objectives/Progress Markers/Benchmarks — Goal

**Student:** *Jake*

**Date:** *Sept. 1, '04*

*Copy sent to parent at end of grading period:* (1) 2 3 4

**PLOP:** *Reads 3rd grade material orally at 80-100 cwpm.*[11]

| **Benchmarks for Marking Periods 1-3** *(last period benchmark is the annual goal)* | **Actual Level Reached**[12] |
|---|---|
| **1.** *3rd grade material at 100-120 cwpm.* <br> **2.** *4th grade material at 80-100 cwpm.* <br> **3.** *4th grade material at 100-120 cwpm.* <br> **4.** *5th grade material at 110-130 cwpm.* | **1.** *3rd grade material read at 98, 92 and 105 cwpm (3 samples).* |

**Services:** *Small group (2-4) instruction daily for 45 minutes in corrective Reading (SRA) plus daily timed and recorded one minute samples, done with peer.*

---

11. Many reading experts prefer to designate correct words per minute and not specify number of errors.
12. If benchmark is significantly exceeded or missed, revise remaining benchmarks appropriately.
Actual level reached for last marking period is the PLOP for next year's IEP, if needed. Notice how the IDEA-mandated progress reporting is simply built into this form. No further effort is required.

*Form 2*

| PLOP | Service to be Provided | Progress Markers | Level Reached Each Grading Period[13] |
|---|---|---|---|
| Has never used a communication board | Direct instruction and positive reinforcement<br><br>15 minutes daily instruction plus use throughout the day | 1. Consistently use 5 symbols<br><br>2. 10 symbols<br><br>3. 15 symbols<br><br>4. 40 symbols (Goal) | 1.<br><br>2.<br><br>3.<br><br>4. |
| Never indicates need to use the bathroom | Modeling to Use sign for toilet plus positive reinforcement for approximation and success | 1. Use sign for toilet when requested/ prompted.<br><br>2. Use sign for toilet appropriately<br><br>3. Maintain<br><br>4. Maintain | 1.<br><br>2.<br><br>3.<br><br>4. |

---

13. This column fulfills the progress assessment/reporting requirement of IDEA.

Note how simple these forms make it to do the mandatory progress reporting to parents. On form 1, our 1st report period objective was for Jake to read his 3rd grade text material at 100-120 cwpm. We spend 3 minutes listening to him read aloud, noting his rate and errors, obtain the one minute rate, jot the result on the form under "Actual level achieved," have the aide copy the form for the parent, and we're done. And we did it in a way that was simple, honest, timely, legally correct and educationally useful. It doesn't get much better than that.

As you examine the 75 sample PLOP — Objectives/Benchmarks/Progress Markers — Goal sequences in the next section, please note the matrix which allows you to quickly find the samples most closely related to your own work. However, the format of other sequences will also be applicable to your needs. Some of these samples fit the ladder model, others the pie. We urge you to examine how these samples could best be incorporated into the IEP form that you use. If that task is difficult, perhaps the form you use should be revised.

Part III:
Sample
Best Practice
PLOPs,
Objectives,
Goals

# Acknowledgement

The authors would like to acknowledge the work of graduate students in Dr. Herr's summer, 2002 Law & Special Education class in developing the PLOPs, goals and objectives that are included in the following section.

## Matrix of PLOPs/Objectives/Goals

| | Early Childhood/Preschool Developmental ages 0 - 5 | Primary/Elementary Developmental ages 6 - 11 | Middle School/High School/Post School Developmental ages 12 - 18 |
|---|---|---|---|
| Access to General Curriculum | 43 | 6, 12, 37, 74, 75 | 14, 30, 33, 49, 54, 62, 74 |
| Reading (decoding, fluency, comprehension) | 17 | 1, 2, 7, 15, 26, 48, 51,74 | 3, 74 |
| Mathematics | 29, 39 | 4, 22, 23, 39, 46, 50, 52 | |
| Written Language | 32 | 32, 36, 44, 53, 58, 72 | 30, 31, 49, 57, 64, 73 |
| Behavioral/Social | 43 | 6, 8, 12, 19, 37, 41, 71 | 33, 41, 62 |
| Expressive/Receptive oral/aural Language | 5, 9, 10, 16, 17, 18, 35 | 13, 26, 35, 40 | 27 |
| Physical (fine, gross motor) | 11, 24, 25, 28, 38, 47, 55 | 42, 45, 56, 63, 66 | |
| Vocational & Pre-vocational | | | 20, 21, 31, 49, 57, 61, 65, 67, 69, 72 |
| Special Education Curriculum (including self-help and functional academics) | 11, 18 | 4, 22, 23, 45, 56, 59, 66, 71 | 31, 34, 60, 61, 68, 70, 72, 73 |

Note: Numbers reflect sample PLOPs, objectives and goals, #1-75, on which subjects in left column are addressed. Items may appear in more than 1 category on age/grade column.

# Present Levels of Performance

Jay is a non-reader who knows no sound-symbol relationships. In print, he recognizes his name and the words "Coca Cola" and "Nike."

# Objectives

1. Given vowels, consonants, digraphs, and 5 common diphthongs, Jay will say the correct sounds at 30 sounds per minute with no more than 2 errors.

2. Given the 200 most common sight vocabulary words, Jay will read them aloud at 110 wpm with only random error.

3. Given first grade material, Jay will read a passage orally at 50-80 wpm with no more than 5 errors.

# Goal

Given first grade material, Jay will read a passage orally at 110-130 wpm with only random errors.

# Present Levels Of Performance

Given third grade material, Walter reads 50-70 wpm with 4-6 errors.

# Objectives

1. Given third grade material, Walter will read 110 120 wpm with 1-3 errors.

2. Given fourth grade material, Walter will read 70-100 wpm with 1-3 errors.

3. Given fifth grade material, Walter will read 70-100 wpm with 1-3 errors.

# Goal

Given fifth grade material, Walter will read 120 wpm with only random error.

# Present Levels of Performance

Given 3 paragraphs of expository reading material, Emily can decode fluently and accurately (at least 100 wpm with random error) but is unable to state or write the main idea and two supporting details for each paragraph.

# Objectives

1. Given 3 paragraphs of expository reading material which Emily can decode fluently and accurately (at least 100 wpm with random error), she will state or write the topic sentence of each paragraph.

2. Given 3 paragraphs of expository reading material which Emily can decode fluently and accurately (at least 100 wpm with random error), she will state or write the main idea of each paragraph.

3. Given 3 paragraphs of expository reading material which Emily can decode fluently and accurately (at least 100 wpm with random error), she will state or write the main idea of the paragraph and one detail for each paragraph.

# Goal

Given 3 paragraphs of expository reading material which Emily can decode fluently and accurately (at least 100 wpm with random error), she will state or write the main idea and two supporting details for each paragraph.

Comment: Students should not be expected to comprehend written material unless they can decode the material easily and accurately.

# Present Levels of Performance

Carol does not tell time.

# Objectives

1. Given pictures of clock faces with the short hand pointing to an hour, Carol will state the hour and also demonstrate that she can count to 60 by 5s, 9 out of 10 trials.

2. Given pictures of clock faces with the long hand pointing to the half hour, Carol will state the time by saying the hour and the word thirty (e.g., seven-thirty) and demonstrate, by showing the direction on the clock, the rule that the clock hands always move in a "clockwise" direction, 9 out of 10 trials.

3. Given pictures of clock faces with the long hand pointing to the quarter hour, Carol will state the time by saying the hour and the words "fifteen" or "forty-five" (e.g., two-fifteen or eight forty-five) and state the rule "Short hand points, long hand counts."

# Goal

Given pictures of clock faces with the hands in any position, Carol will state the correct time in "minutes after the hour," accurate to the nearest 5 minutes, 9 of 10 trials.

# Present Levels of Performance

Emil promptly follows simple, one-step directions such as "Touch the block" or "sit down" fewer than 1 of 5 times.

# Objectives

1. Given a one-step direction, Emil will promptly follow the direction 9 out of 10 times.

2. Given a two-step direction, Emil will promptly follow at least the first of the two steps 9 out of 10 times.

3. Given a two-step direction, Emil will promptly follow both directions 9 out of 10 times.

# Goal

Give a three-step direction, Emil will promptly follow all three steps, in the correct order, 9 out of 10 times.

# Present Levels of Performance

Gerry completes and submits fewer than half of his homework assignments.

# Objectives

1. Gerry will submit at least 6 of 10 assignments.

2. Gerry will submit at least 8 of 10 assignments.

3. Gerry will submit 10 of 10 assignments.

# Goal

Given homework assignments within his academic capabilities, Gerry will continue to complete and submit each assignment at a level judged as satisfactory by his teacher.

# Present Levels of Performance

Given unlimited time and the Dolch 110 easy sight words, Hatsuko reads 20-30 correctly.
She has particular difficulty with certain words: when, where, they, there, then, who, what.

# Objectives

1. Hatsuko will read 50 Dolch words correctly.

2. Hatsuko will read 70 Dolch words correctly.

3. Hatsuko will read 90 Dolch words correctly.

# Goal

Hatsuko will read all 110 Dolch sight words in 1 minute with no more than random error.

# Present Levels of Performance

During free time such as lunch or recess, Ivy always runs away when approached by a peer.

# Objectives

1. During free time such as lunch or recess, Ivy will stand still and look at peers who approach her 3 out of 5 days.

2. During free time such as lunch or recess, Ivy will stand still, look at peers who approach her, and say, "hi" 3 out of 5 days.

3. During free time such as lunch or recess, Ivy will approach at least one other peer and say, "Hi" 3 out of 5 days.

# Goal

During free time such as lunch or recess, Ivy will interact appropriately with peers who approach her or will initiate an interaction with at least one other peer and say, "hi" every day.

# Present Levels of Performance

When given common objects or pictures, Abel correctly points only to "dog," "kitty," and "truck".

# Objectives

1. When given common objects or pictures, Abel will correctly point to 15 of them.

2. When given 30 common objects or pictures, Abel will correctly point to 30 of them.

3. When given common objects or pictures, Abel will correctly point to 60 of them.

# Goal

When given common objects or pictures, Abel will correctly point to 100 of them.

# Present Levels of Performance

Bonnie does not imitate simple gestures or sounds.

# Objectives

1. When prompted verbally with the words, "Do this" followed by a gesture, Bonnie will correctly imitate at least 5 different gestures.

2. When prompted verbally with the words, "say this" followed by a sound, Bonnie will correctly imitate at least 5 different sounds.

3. When prompted verbally with the words, "Do this" followed by a gesture, Bonnie will correctly imitate any modeled gesture.

4. When prompted verbally with the words, "say this" followed by a sound, Bonnie will correctly imitate any modeled sound.

# Goal

When prompted verbally, Bonnie will correctly imitate any simple gesture or sound that is modeled for her.

# Present Levels of Performance

Carly passively cooperates when being dressed but does not dress herself or take any initiative in assisting getting herself dressed.

# Objectives

1. When prompted verbally, Carly will put her arms in the sleeves of a shirt so that someone else can pull her shirt on and will lift one foot at a time and put it in the correct leg of her pants when someone holds them for her.

2. When prompted verbally, Carly will put her arms in the sleeves and her head through the neck hole of a shirt and pull the shirt down when someone holds the shirt for her and will lift one foot at a time and put it in the correct leg of her pants and pull the pants up when someone holds them for her.

3. When prompted verbally and handed her clothes one item at a time, Carly will pull on underwear, a pullover shirt, and elastic waist pants on her own.

# Goal

Without prompting, Carly will dress herself in underwear, shirt, pants, socks and shoes when an outfit has been laid out for her ahead of time.

# Present Levels of Performance

Dani averaged 20 unexcused absences and 12 tardies per grading period last year.

# Objectives

1. Dani will attend school at least 30 days and be on time to all of her classes on at least 25 of those days during the first 9-week grading period.

2. Dani will attend school at least 35 days and be on time to all of her classes on at least 32 of those days during the second 9-week grading period.

3. Dani will attend school at least 40 days and be on time to all of her classes on at least 38 of those days during the third 9-week grading period.

# Goal

Dani will attend school every day and be on time for all of her classes during the final 9-week grading period.

# Present Levels of Performance

Edie has had no exposure to a "picture activity schedule" and has never responded to one.

# Objectives

1. Given a single picture task, Edie will look at the picture, get any necessary items, perform the depicted task, and put the items away with no assistance and no more than one re-direction.

2. Given a two-picture task, Edie will look at each picture, get any necessary items, perform each depicted task, and put the items away with no assistance and no more than one re-direction.

3. Given a three-picture task, Edie will look at each picture, get any necessary items, perform each depicted task, and put the items away with no assistance and no more than one re-direction.

# Goal

Given a four-picture task, Edie will look at each picture, get any necessary items, perform each depicted tasks, and put the items away with no assistance and no more than one re-direction.

# Present Levels of Performance

Each of Frances' teachers reports that she "almost never" (less than once a week) comes to class with her homework ready to turn in, the right book, and pen and notebook.

# Objectives

1. Frances will come to classes prepared (with homework, book, pen and notebook) 4 out of 5 days 3 consecutive weeks.

2. Frances will come to classes prepared (with homework, book, pen, and notebook) 9 out of 10 days for 3 consecutive two-week periods.

3. Frances will come to classes prepared (with homework, book, pen, and notebook) 19 out of 20 days for two consecutive months.

# Goal

Frances will come to classes fully prepared every day.

# Present Levels of Performance

Given unfamiliar material from a 4th grade level text, Joan orally reads 40-50 wpm with 4-7 errors.

# Objectives

1. Given unfamiliar material from a 4th grade level text, Joan orally reads 80-100 wpm with 0-3 errors.

2. Given unfamiliar material from a 5th grade level text, Joan orally reads 100-120 wpm with 0-2 errors.

3. Given unfamiliar material from a 6th grade level text, Joan orally reads 120-140 wpm with 0-2 errors.

# Goal

Given unfamiliar material from a 6th grade level text, Joan orally reads 150-180 wpm with 0-2 errors.

# Present Levels of Performance

When asked his name, address, and telephone number, Danny does not answer.

# Objectives

1. When asked his name, Danny will always respond correctly.

2. When asked his address, Danny will always respond correctly.

3. When asked his telephone number, Danny will always respond correctly.

# Goal

When asked his name, address, and telephone number, Danny will answer all three correctly every time.

# Present Levels of Performance

Heather does not rhyme, blend sounds or segment words.

# Objectives

1. Given any one syllable word (real or nonsense), Heather will immediately respond with two or more rhyming words (real or nonsense) on 9 of 10 trials.

2. Given three phonemes (sounds) in a CVC order, one sound at a time at a rate of one second per sound, Heather will blend them into the correct word and say it at normal speed, 9 of 10 trials.

3. Given a one syllable word (CVC), Heather will say the phonemes (sounds) separately, in correct order in 9 of 10 trials.

# Goal

Given stimulus words/sounds, Heather will rhyme, blend sounds, and segment words correctly on 9 of 10 trials.

# Present Levels of Performance

Angela can say her first name when prompted but does not state her last name, her address, or her phone number when prompted.

# Objectives

1. When prompted verbally, Angela will state both her first and last name on 5 out of 5 trials on 3 consecutive days.

2. When prompted verbally, Angela will state her complete address on 5 out of 5 trials on 3 consecutive days.

3. When prompted verbally, Angela will recite her phone number on 5 out of 5 trials on 3 consecutive days.

# Goal

When prompted verbally, Angela will state both her first and last name, her address, and her phone number on 5 out of 5 trials on 3 consecutive days.

# Present Levels of Performance

Bethany looks down at the ground when an individual approaches her and starts talking to her, moves 2 feet or more away from the person, and doesn't respond when the person introduces himself/herself.

# Objectives

1. Bethany will stay or move to within one foot of a person who initiates a verbal interaction with her.

2. Bethany will maintain eye contact with another individual as long as that person is talking to her.

3. When someone introduces himself or herself to Bethany by saying, "Hi, my name is _____", Bethany will look the person in the eye and respond by saying, "Hi, my name is Bethany."

# Goal

Bethany will stay or move to within one foot of a person who initiates a verbal interaction with her, will maintain eye contact as long as that person is talking to her, and will respond to introductions by looking the person in the eye and saying, "Hi, my name is Bethany.

# Present Levels of Performance

Donna is a 10th grader who has no idea what she wants to do after high school. She says she wants to get a job, but she doesn't know what kind of work she would enjoy doing.

# Objectives

1. Donna will attend the job fair that is held every November in her high school and gather brochures from each of the venders. After the fair, Donna will read each brochure and choose the 3 jobs that most appeal to her.

2. With the assistance of her school counselor or the school vocational coordinator, Donna will contact a community representative for each of the 3 jobs that caught her interest at the job fair and will arrange to visit each person's place of work for a day. While visiting each site, Donna will find out and record (tape or in writing) what kind of education and training a person needs in order to be eligible for an entry-level position in that particular job.

3. With the assistance of a school counselor, Donna will use resources such as the Dictionary of Occupational Titles and the computerized Career Information System to look up each of these three jobs she observed and find out what the demand is for each job in her local community and in her state.

# Goal

Donna will investigate three jobs which interest her and find out what kind of education and training is required for each job and also find out what demand there is in her community and her state for each job.

# Present Levels of Performance

Albert has no paid work experience and has had little responsibility for chores at home. Although willing to comply with requests for help at home, Albert shows little initiative to find or complete tasks independently.

# Objectives

1. Albert will initiate and complete two daily chores (making his bed and putting away the dinner dishes) and two weekly chores (taking out the garbage and cleaning his room) at home. Daily chores will be completed 5 out of 7 days, and weekly chores 3 out of 4 weeks.

2. While continuing to maintain his chores at home, Albert will also work in the school library, reshelving books, for three hours a week. Albert will report to the librarian every Monday, Wednesday, and Friday between 2 and 3 pm, will locate the cart with books that need to be reshelved, and will work at reshelving the books with no reminders to stay on task for 2 of the 3 days each week.

3. While continuing to maintain his chores at home, Albert will work in the student-run coffee cart business at school for 2 _ hours a week (30 minutes each day before classes begin). He will be responsible for stocking the supply shelves and clearing and cleaning the tables in the student area. The coffee cart supervisor will check Albert's work daily and complete the "worker checklist" that is used with all student workers. Albert will earn 100% on 4 out of 5 days.

# Goal

Albert will demonstrate good work habits by initiating and completing 2 daily and 3 weekly chores at home, reshelving books at the school library for 3 hours a week without reminders to stay on task, and restock shelves and clear and clean tables according to the "Worker Checklist" in the student area at school $2\frac{1}{2}$ hours a week.

# Present Levels of Performance

Cheri does not know how to count change consisting of a mixture of quarters, dimes, nickels, and pennies. She can identify individual coins by name and can count by 1s, 5s, and 10s to 100.

# Objectives

1. Cheri will count quarters (by 25s) to $1.00 on 9 out of 10 trials for 5 consecutive days.

2. Cheri will count nickels (by 5s) to $1.00 beginning at any number than ends with 0 or 5 on 9 out of 10 trials for 5 consecutive days.

3. Cheri will count various amounts of money <$1.00 created with quarters and nickels on 9 out of 10 trials for 5 consecutive days.

4. Cheri will count dimes (by 10s) to $1.00 beginning at any number than ends with 0 or 5 up to 100 on 9 out of 10 trials for 5 consecutive days.

5. Cheri will count various amounts of money <$1.00 created with quarters, nickels, and dimes on 9 out of 10 trials for 5 consecutive days.

6. Cheri will count pennies (by 1s) to $1.00 beginning with any number that ends with 0 or 5 on 9 out of 10 trials for 5 consecutive days.

# Goal

Cheri will count various amounts of money, all less than $1.00, created with quarters, nickels, dimes and pennies.

# Present Levels of Performance

Daniel doesn't know how to use a calendar.

# Objectives

1. Given a specific month of the year, either verbally or in writing, Daniel will turn to that month using a current year calendar which has one page for each month on 8 out of 10 trials.

2. Given a specific month of the year and a specific date of the month (e.g., March 23), either verbally or in writing, Daniel will turn to the correct month using a current year calendar which has one page for each month and point to the correct date on 8 out of 10 trials.

3. Using a current year calendar which has one page for each month, Daniel will correctly identify the current date, yesterday's date, and tomorrow's date and tell the day of the week on which each falls on 8 out of 10 trials.

# Goal

Daniel will correctly locate any date on a current year calendar which has one page for each month, as well as be able to locate today's date, yesterday's date, and tomorrow's date on the calendar and tell the day of the week on which the requested date falls on 8 out of 10 trials.

# Present Levels of Performance

Andra, who is two years, 10 months old, was raised in a crib in an Eastern European orphanage and never learned to walk or crawl, but he does stand holding onto the crib railing.

# Objectives

1. When placed on the floor, Andra will crawl to reach a toy that is 3 feet away from him.

2. When someone holds his hands and walks behind him, Andra will walk across a room that is 10 feet wide.

3. Andra will walk without assistance with only occasional falls.

# Goal

Andra will walk and run freely and independently.

# Present Levels of Performance

Shandra completes a three piece (circle, square, triangle) form board with assistance.

# Objectives

1. Given a wooden puzzle board with shape cutouts (animals, people, or common objects), with each cutout separated from the others, and given the appropriate puzzle pieces, Shandra will put the puzzle pieces in the correct cutouts without assistance on 9 out of 10 trials.

2. Given any of several child's jigsaw puzzles that each have just 5 large puzzle pieces, Shandra will construct the puzzle without assistance on 9 out of 10 trials.

3. Given any child's jigsaw puzzle with up to 10 puzzle pieces, Shandra will construct the puzzle without assistance on 9 out of 10 trials.

# Goal

Given any child's jigsaw puzzle with 10 -20 puzzle pieces, Shandra will construct the puzzle without assistance on 9 out of 10 trials.

# Present Levels of Performance

Matti substitutes the /p/ sound for the letter /f/ and the /d/ sound for the letter /j/ when these letters appear in the beginning, medial and final positions in words.

# Objectives

1. Matti will correctly say the /f/ sound, with prompting, whenever it appears in words Matti is asked to read.

2. Matti will correctly say the /j/ sound, with prompting, whenever it appears in words Matti is asked to read.

3. Matti will correctly say both the /f/ and /j/ sounds, with prompting, whenever they appear in words Matti is asked to read.

# Goal

Matti will correctly and without prompting say the /f/ and /j/ sounds whenever they appear in words Matti is asked to read.

# Present Levels of Performance

Buddy has difficulty remembering/retrieving what he has studied, heard or seen. For example, when shown a magazine cover with 24 objects depicted, he was able to recall only two objects five minutes later. After studying a map showing ten major U.S. rivers, he could label only one correctly. He has no "system" to help him recall specifics.

# Objectives

1. Given lists of words which can be arranged so that the first letter of each word makes a common word (i.e., the mnemonic word), Buddy will write the mnemonic word on paper, arrange the words on the list in the mnemonic order, and study the words until he can recite the word list with 90% accuracy.

2. Given a page of common objects which can be categorized by use (e.g., tools, foods, clothing), Buddy will write down the categories and list the objects that fit each category. He will then study each category until he can list all of the objects from memory with 90% accuracy.

3. Given a list of 10 names, labels, or objects, Buddy will use a mnemonic system to memorize the information. He will study the information for 15 minutes at a time until he can recall the information with 80% accuracy after time periods of 1 hour, 3 hours and 6 hours.

# Goal

Given 15 minutes to study, Buddy will recall 8 of 10 names, labels, or objects a day after learning them, using at least 2 different mnemonic association methods.

# Present Levels of Performance

On the ABC Fine Motor Development Subtest given in September, 6 year old Annie scored at the $4\frac{1}{2}$ year old level.

# Objectives

1. Given tracing paper, a pattern (simply drawn objects, letters or numbers ), and a pencil, Annie will trace the pattern without deviating from the pattern by more than $\frac{1}{8}$ inch at any point in her tracing.

2. Given a design (simply drawn objects, letters or numbers ), paper and a pencil, Annie will accurately copy the design on her paper.

3. Given a simple line drawing or picture, Annie will use safety scissors to cut out the drawing/picture without deviating from the lines by more than $\frac{1}{8}$ inch at any point.

# Goal

When given the ABC Fine Motor Development Subtest in December, Annie will score at the $5\frac{1}{2}$ year old level.

# Present Levels of Performance

Madison does not count objects, count by rote, recognize numerals or match numbers and objects.

# Objectives

1. Madison will count by rote from 1 to 100 without prompting and with 100% accuracy.

2. Madison will correctly identify the numerals 0-20 with 100% accuracy.

3. Madison will count up to 20 objects using one-to-one correspondence with 100% accuracy.

4. Madison will count by twos and fives from 0 to 100 with 100% accuracy.

# Goal

Madison will count by ones, twos, and fives from 0 to 100, name numerals and match number and objects to 20.

# Present Levels of Performance

Mark's best written report to date consists of two paragraphs copied almost verbatim from an encyclopedia. Mark knows how to search the internet for information on topics he is given.

# Objectives

1. Given a specific topic and question to answer, Mark will search the internet for information that addresses the topic and the question. Mark will print one article about the topic from each of 5 different websites.

2. Given the articles from a web search, Mark will read each article and take written notes of the information that pertains to his topic and topic question, putting the information in his own words in each case.

3. Given his written notes from 5 internet articles, Mark will compare and contrast the information and create an outline or graphic map of the information he wants to include in a written report.

# Goal

Given a topic and internet access, Mark will prepare a report of at least 500 words using at least 5 sources.

# Present Levels of Performance

Jodi is completely unfamiliar with computers, including keyboards.

# Objectives

1. Using a computer typing program such as "Maevis Beacon Teaches Typing" (TLC Multimedia, Inc.) or "Type to Learn" (Sunburst Technology Corp.) to learn keyboarding skills, Jodi will type at a rate of at least 35 wpm with 4 or fewer errors.

2. Using a widely available word processing program such as Microsoft Word or Corel WordPerfect, Jodi will demonstrate that she can type an already prepared essay on the computer, name the file, and save it to a floppy disk or the hard disk of the computer.

3. Using the same word processing program, Jodi will demonstrate that she can open a file which she has previously saved, edit the file, save her changes and print the file.

# Goal

Using word processing software on a computer, Jodi will compose a 5 paragraph essay, save the essay, retrieve the essay and revise it, checking for spelling and grammar errors, save the revised essay and print it.

# Present Levels of Performance

Nicholas does not generate or legibly copy any letters or numbers.

# Objectives

1. Given a pencil and lined paper with partial images of letters (in manuscript form) and numbers and correct models, Nicholas will accurately trace the letters and numbers.

2. Given a model of the letters of the alphabet and the numerals 0-9, a pencil, and lined paper, Nicholas will accurately copy all of the letters and numerals without assistance.

3. Given a model of his printed name, Nicholas will accurately copy his name without assistance.

# Goal

Without models, Nicholas will legibly print his name, all letters of the alphabet, and the numerals 0-9 in less than 2 minutes.

# Present Levels of Performance

Jason is blind and has just entered a large, urban (2000 students) middle school. He is completely unfamiliar with the campus.

# Objectives

1. With a peer as a verbal guide, Jason will get off the school bus and walk to the office and from there to any of the four buildings on campus.

2. With a peer as a verbal guide, Jason will navigate between his classes throughout his daily schedule of courses and board the bus at the end of the day.

3. Without peer support, Jason will get off the school bus and walk to his first period class. With a peer to offer verbal assistance only if Jason becomes confused, he will navigate between classes to his next classroom.

# Goal

Jason will get off the school bus in the morning and independently walk from that area to the school office and then to any of the four buildings of the middle school complex. He will navigate independently between his classes whether he is going to lunch, P.E. or any one of his other classes and board the correct bus at the end of the day.

# Present Levels of Performance

Zachary is 16 years old. He can read simple menus, write basic sight words and copy any word he reads. He uses the next-dollar strategy to pay for things he buys. Zachary can follow simple recipes to prepare dinner foods.

# Objectives

1. Given a menu of dinners for one week, Zachary will identify and make a list of the foods he would need to purchase in order to prepare those menus.

2. Given grocery store ads from several different stores and a list of foods he needs to purchase, Zachary will compare the prices of foods on the list that are on sale at each grocery store, and write the name of the store that has the best price for each item.

3. Given all of the above information, Zachary will make a list of foods to purchase from each store according to which store has the best price for a particular food item, and determine which store has the most food items on the list for the best price.

# Goal

Given a menu of simple dinners for the week, Zachary will make a list of the food items he will need to purchase, examine the grocery store ads from the local newspaper, and determine which store has the best prices for most of the items he needs. He will record the store price next to each food item on his list, use a calculator to find the total cost, and determine how much money he needs to take to the grocery store.

# Present Levels of Performance

Vera is non-verbal and has never used a language board or other assistive technology device to communicate her needs, preferences, or to give or respond to simple greetings.

# Objectives

1. With the assistance of the assistive technology specialist, Vera will try out different communication systems which vary in ease of use (e.g., simple language boards with just a few pictures to which Vera can point; switch-driven computerized communication devices on which Vera can choose from a successive variety of screens of pictures and/or words) to determine the highest level of communication board which Vera can use successfully and with maximum independence.

2. With initial instruction from an assistive technology specialist and assistance when needed from an instructional aide, Vera will use the chosen communication system to indicate a variety of needs (e.g., use the bathroom, drink or eat, go outside, take a short break from work) and her preferences for classroom activities.

3. With limited assistance from an instructional aide, Vera will use the chosen communication system to initiate or respond to verbal interactions from her teachers, aides, and classmates.

# Goal

Vera will use the chosen assistive technology device to express her needs, preferences, and to initiate or respond to verbal interactions from her teachers, aides, and classmates.

# Present Levels of Performance

Given a story starter, Bart writes one sentence or less (usually 3 - 8 words) and makes approximately twice as many errors (spacing, spelling, letter formations) as he has words.

# Objectives

1. Bart will successfully complete (according to the program criteria) lessons 1 - 40 of the Expressive Writing program (SRA Publishers).

2. Bart will successfully complete (according to the program criteria) lessons 41 - 80 of the Expressive Writing program (SRA Publishers).

3. Bart will successfully complete (according to the program criteria) lessons 81 - 120 of the Expressive Writing program (SRA Publishers).

# Goal

Given a story starter, Bart will write a story that contains at least 10 sentences with no more than 10 errors of spelling, punctuation or grammar.

# Present Levels of Performance

Jessica does not participate appropriately in small group (2 - 5 students) projects. She always disrupts and then leaves the group, usually with highly inappropriate comments (e.g., "You idiots," "Why can't you do it right?") to other group members.

# Objectives

1. When prompted, Jessica will make positive statements about other students in her class on at least 9 of 10 trials.

2. When assigned to a small group to work on a project, Jessica will remain with the group for the entire time and will make only positive statements to the other group members on 9 of 10 trials.

3. When assigned to a small group to work on a project, Jessica will make positive comments to the other members of the group, will make positive suggestions to contribute to the project work, and will remain with the group on 9 of 10 trials.

# Goal

In 9 of 10 opportunities, Jessica will participate appropriately and cooperatively and will remain with the group and contribute to the project.

# Present Levels of Performance

At the age of 10, Danny goes up and down stairs by putting both feet on each step before moving on to the next step, does not catch a large (8" diameter) ball tossed to him gently from 10 feet away, and cannot insert a key into his front door lock to unlock the door.

# Objectives

1. Danny will walk up and down stairs by alternating feet on alternate steps without assistance on 10 of 10 trials.

2. Danny will use both hands to catch a large ball tossed to him from 10 feet away on 8 of 10 trials.

3. When Danny gets home from school each day, he will use his house key, which he carries on a lanyard, to unlock his front door on the first trial each day.

# Goal

Danny will use a normal gait to walk up or down stairs, will catch a large ball, and will be able to unlock his front door.

# Present Levels of Performance

Rhonda does not count objects, present or not present. She does not count by rote.

# Objectives

1. Rhonda will accurately count up to 10 by rote and will be able to accurately count up to 10 objects which are present and which she can touch (e.g., blocks, books, pencils).

2. Rhonda will accurately count up to 20 by rote and will be able to accurately count up to 10 objects which are present but which she does not touch (e.g., number of people in her reading group, number of coins on the table).

3. Rhonda will accurately count up to five objects which were present and then report the number of objects after they are removed (e.g, students in line who then leave the classroom; blocks on a table that are then put away in a cupboard).

# Goal

When asked to count 0-5 events or objects not present (e.g., How many visitors came to our room yesterday? How many times did I clap my hands? How many words did I just say?) Rhonda will do so with only random error.

# Present Levels of Performance

Abby rarely sequences the telling of stories, giving directions, or making explanations so that they are clear to the listener. When she gave a report to her 25 classmates on how to bathe a dog, only 2 students believed the steps had been presented in a logical sequence.

# Objectives

1. After listening to a story in which there were three sequential events, Abby will state, when prompted, what happened first, what happened second and what happened third. She will correctly identify the order on 8 out of 10 trials.

2. Given 5 sentence strips, in mixed order, which create a story with a beginning, middle and end when the sentences are put in the correct order, Abby will put the sentence strips in an order that makes sense on 8 of 10 trials. She will then read the story out loud.

3. When given a task to describe, such as bathing the dog, making a peanut butter and jelly sandwich, Abby will identify what step should be completed first, second, third, etc., until the task is complete. She will suggest a feasible sequence of steps on 8 of 10 trials.

# Goal

Given an unfamiliar short story or video drama or a familiar task, Abby will be able to tell the sequence well enough that 20 of the 25 classmates will agree that the order made sense.

# Present Levels of Performance

Bruce responds to teasing from his classmates by loud name calling, yelling, and making somewhat bizarre movements intended to be threatening but which have the effect of eliciting more teasing. The teasing-response sequence occurs several times daily.

# Objectives

1. In a role playing situation, Bruce will demonstrate walking away quietly when an instructional assistant models teasing him by saying something like, "Show me what you would do if I said your shirt was ugly." Bruce will walk away 9 times out of 10.

2. On the playground, Bruce will always walk away without saying anything when a classmate teases him. He will walk to the instructional assistant on duty and say, "I walked away when I was teased."

3. On the playground, Bruce will always walk away without saying anything and will keep his hands at his sides or in his pants pockets when a classmate teases him. He will walk to the instructional assistant on duty and say, "I walked away when I was teased and I kept my hands in my pockets/at my side."

# Goal

When Bruce is teased by classmates, he will walk away and ignore the teasing every time without having to report his success in handling the situation to anyone.

# Present Levels of Performance

Jane cuts paper awkwardly using scissors.

# Objectives

1. Given scissors and a paper marked with two straight lines 3 inches apart, Jane will cut the paper between two straight lines on 4 of 5 trials.

2. Given scissors and a paper marked with two straight lines 1 inch apart, Jane will cut the paper between two straight lines on 4 of 5 trials.

3. Given scissors and a paper marked with two straight lines $1/2$ inch apart, Jane will cut the paper between two straight lines on 4 of 5 trials.

# Goal

Given scissors and a paper marked with two straight lines $1/4$ inch apart, Jane will cut the paper between two straight lines on 4 of 5 trials.

# Present Levels of Performance

Jen does not share toys with her classmates in free play time at preschool.

# Objectives

1. Given a teacher's physical and verbal reinforcement, Jen shares toys with her classmates in free play time on 3 of 5 consecutive play periods.

2. Given a teacher's verbal reinforcement, Jen shares toys with her classmates in free play time on 4 of 5 consecutive play periods.

3. Without any prompting, Jen shares toys with her classmates in free play time on 4 of 5 consecutive play periods.

# Goal

Jen always shares toys with her classmates in free play time.

# Present Levels of Performance

When prompted, David can write all letters of the alphabet with an average of six errors in alphabetical order.

# Objectives

1. When prompted David will write all letters of the alphabet in the correct order with less than five errors.

2. When prompted, David will write all letters of the alphabet in the correct order with less than four errors.

3. When prompted, David will write all letters of the alphabet in the correct order with less than two errors.

# Goal

When prompted, David will write the letters of the alphabet in the correct order with no errors.

# Present Levels of Performance

Amy always requires reminding when her shoes need to be tied and always requires assistance tying her shoes.

# Objectives

1. When prompted, Amy will tie her shoes with minimal assistance.

2. When prompted, Amy will tie her shoes without assistance.

3. Amy will tie her shoes without assistance and without prompting 3 of every 4 mornings.

# Goal

Amy always ties her shoes without prompting and without assistance any time her shoes come untied.

# Present Levels of Performance

Juan needs to use a multiplication chart or a calculator when multiplying one digit numbers.

# Objectives

1. Juan will use a calculator or a multiplication chart only when multiplying single digit numbers greater than three.

2. Juan will use a calculator or a multiplication chart only when multiplying single digit numbers greater than six.

3. Juan will use a calculator or a multiplication chart only when multiplying single digit numbers greater than nine.

# Goal

Juan will never use a multiplication chart or calculator when multiplying single digit numbers.

# Present Levels of Performance

Carl is a 5th grade student who has CP, and just had surgery over the summer to help him with his ability to walk. At this point he can walk approximately 5 steps independently before falling.

# Objectives

1. At the end of the first nine weeks, Carl will be able to walk 15 yards independently without falling.

2. At the end of the second nine weeks, Carl will be able to walk 25 yards independently without falling.

3. At the end of the third nine weeks, Carl will be able to walk 40 yards independently without falling.

# Goal

By June 1st, Carl will be able to walk independently across a level surface for 50 yards without falling.

# Present Levels of Performance

Jane is a 4th grade student who reads 3rd grade material aloud at a rate of 50-60 wpm with 7-12 mistakes.

# Objectives

1. At the end of the first nine weeks Jane will read 3rd grade text at a rate of 70-80 wpm with no more than 5 errors.

2. At the end of the second nine weeks, Jane will read 3rd grade text at a rate of 100-110 wpm with no more than 2 errors.

3. At the end of the third nine weeks Jane will read 4th grade text at a rate of 50-60 wpm with no more than 2 errors.

# Goal

By the end of the school year Jane will be able to read 4th grade text at a rate of 70-90 wpm with no more than 2 errors.

# Present Levels of Performance

Billy is an 11th grader who wants to attend college after graduation. He currently has limited keyboarding skills. He types approximately 20 wpm with 8-12 errors.

# Objectives

1. Billy will practice his keyboarding skills using Mavis Beacon computer typing program and will type at least 35 wpm with no more than 3 errors by the end of the first nine week period.

2. Billy will practice his keyboarding skills using Mavis Beacon computer typing program and will type at least 45 wpm with no more than 3 errors by the end of the second nine week period.

3. Billy will practice his keyboarding skills using Mavis Beacon computer typing program and will type at least 55 wpm with no more than 3 errors by the end of the third nine week period.

# Goal

By the end of the school year, Billy will type at least 65 wpm with no more than 3 errors.

# Present Levels of Performance

Tanika can recognize and add single digit numbers but cannot subtract or multiply them.

# Objectives

1. When given a page of 30 single digit subtraction problems, Tanika will complete the page in one minute with no more than 2 errors.

2. When given a page of 30 mixed single digit addition and subtraction problems, Tanika will complete the page in one minute with no more than 2 errors.

3. When given a page of 30 single digit multiplication problems, Tanika will complete the page in one minute with no more than 2 errors.

# Goal

When given a page of 30 single digit mixed addition, subtraction and multiplication problems, Tanika will complete the page in one minute with no more than 2 errors.

# Present Levels of Performance

Hannah is currently in second grade. She can read from a first grade basal passage at an average rate of 34 correct words per minute (CWPM) with five errors and from a second grade basal passage at a rate of 30 CWPM with 6 errors.

# Objectives

1. Given a first grade basal, Hannah will orally read at least 50 CWPM with 4 or fewer errors on three consecutive timed readings and when given a second grade basal, Hannah will orally read at least 45 CWPM with 4 or fewer errors on three consecutive timed readings.

2. Given a first grade basal, Hannah will orally read at least 75 CWPM with 4 or fewer errors on three consecutive timed readings and when given a second grade basal, Hannah will orally read at least 60 CWPM with 4 or fewer errors on three consecutive timed readings.

3. Given a second grade basal, Hannah will orally read at least 70 CWPM with 3 or fewer errors on three consecutive timed readings and when given a third grade basal, Hannah will orally read at least 50 CWPM with 5 or fewer errors on three consecutive timed readings.

# Goal

Hannah will orally read from a third grade basal passage at an average rate of at least 70 CWPM with 4 or fewer errors. Hannah's progress will be monitored and measured through weekly timed readings.

# Present Levels of Performance

Treshawn is currently learning to skip count (count by some number to a sum 10 times greater than that number). He can skip count by 2s, 5s, and 10s without error.

# Objectives

1. Treshawn will skip count by 3s and 9s without errors.

2. Treshawn will skip count by 4s and 8s without errors.

3. Treshawn will skip count by 6s and 7s without errors.

# Goal

Given numerals 1-10, Treshawn will skip count up to the x 10 position for each numeral in 20 seconds or less.

# Present Levels of Performance

When writing, Jamie has many great ideas but he does not correctly use capitals at the beginning of each sentence and appropriate end punctuation for each sentence.

# Objectives

1. Jamie will write 5 sentences that begin with a capital letter and end with a period or question mark every day for five consecutive days.

2. When asked to write a paragraph of 3-5 sentences, Jamie will begin each sentence with a capital letter and end each sentence with appropriate punctuation.

3. When asked to write an essay with at least 3 paragraphs, Jamie will begin each sentence with a capital letter and end each sentence with appropriate punctuation.

# Goal

Whenever Jamie completes written assignments, he will begin each sentence with a capital letter and end each sentence with appropriate punctuation.

# Present Levels of Performance

Tracy is an 8th grader who is unable to identify and/or locate most of the 50 states on a map of the United States. She is able to correctly locate California and Oregon.

# Objectives

1. Given a map of the United States with the states outlined but not named, Tracy will correctly write in the names of the Pacific coast states (California, Washington, Oregon), the Rocky Mountain states (Colorado, Idaho, Montana, Nevada, Utah, Wyoming) plus Alaska and Hawaii.

2. Given a map of the United States with the states outlined but not named, Tracy will correctly write in the names of the Southwestern states (Arizona, New Mexico, Oklahoma, Texas), the New England states (Connecticut, Maine, Massachusetts, New Hampshire, Rhode Island, Vermont) and the Middle Atlantic states (New Jersey, New York, and Pennsylvania).

3. Given a map of the United States with the states outlined but not named, Tracy will correctly write in the names of the Southern states (Alabama, Arkansas, Delaware, Florida, Georgia, Kentucky, Louisiana, Maryland, Mississippi, North Carolina, South Carolina, Tennessee, Virginia, West Virginia).

4. Given a map of the United States with the states outlined but not named, Tracy will correctly write in the names of the Midwestern states (Illinois, Indiana, Iowa, Kansas, Michigan, Minnesota, Missouri, Nebraska, North Dakota, Ohio, South Dakota, Wisconsin).

# Goal

Given a map of the United States with the states outlined but not named, Tracy will correctly write in the names of all 50 states.

# Present Levels of Performance

Susan is a 5 year old Kindergartner. She is able to balance and stand on her right foot for 8 seconds at a time. She is not able to balance and stand on her left foot without falling.

# Objectives

1. Susan will use a balance bar to hold onto while she balances on her left foot for 3 seconds.

2. Susan will independently balance on her left foot for 3 seconds without falling.

3. Susan will independently balance on her left foot for 5 seconds without falling.

# Goal

Susan will independently be able to stand on her left foot for 8 seconds and retain her balance without falling.

# Present Levels of Performance

Leticia can use a spoon to feed herself independently. She needs assistance to use a fork and knife to cut large pieces of food, such as meat, that cannot be cut with a spoon.

# Objectives

1. Given a fork, a plate and a piece of meat already precut, Leticia will grasp the fork with her dominant hand, spear the food with the fork and put the food in her mouth without assistance.

2. Given a fork, knife, a dish and food, Leticia will grasp the fork with her non-dominant hand, spear the food with the fork, grasp the knife with her dominant hand, place the knife on food and cut through food without assistance.

3. Given a fork, a knife, a dish and food, Leticia will grasp the fork with her non-dominant hand and spear the food with the fork, grasp the knife with her dominant hand, place the knife on food, cut through food, put the knife on the side of the plate, grasp fork with her dominant hand and transfer the food to her mouth without assistance.

# Goal

Given a fork and a knife, and food on a dish, Leticia will be able use fork and knife successfully to cut large pieces of food into smaller pieces and place food into her mouth without dropping the food. She will do this independently.

# Present Levels of Performance

Jeffery is a high school senior who has difficulty recognizing and correcting spelling and grammar errors in his writing. As part of his transition plan, he is working on completing job applications, his resume and cover/thank you letters. He typically has 5 or more errors present in each such written document after he has completed multiple drafts and proofreading.

# Objectives

1. Given a blank job application to complete, Jeffery will use a cue card which contains his personal information, list of references, and previous experience to complete the application without errors.

2. Given a job application scenario, Jeffery will use a computer and its spell checking and grammar checking features to compose a cover letter and a thank you letter with two or fewer errors.

3. Jeffery will use his job application cue card and a computer and its spell checking and grammar checking features to create a resume with no errors.

# Goal

Jeffery will accurately complete job applications, his resume, and cover letters or thank you letters with correct spelling and grammar.

# Present Levels of Performance

Michael can identify all 26 letters of the alphabet when shown a single letter randomly. He can write 7 letters correctly which are the letters in his name. Michael cannot produce the other 19 letters of the alphabet correctly.

# Objectives

1. Given the letters B, D, F, G, and J, Michael will write each letter with correct line placement in 4 out of 5 consecutive trials.

2. Given the letters K, N, O, P and Q, Michael will write each letter with correct line placement in 4 out of 5 consecutive trials.

3. Given the letters R, S, T, U, and V, Michael will write each letter with correct line placement in 4 out of 5 consecutive trials.

4. Given the letters W, X, Y, and Z, Michael will write each letter with correct line placement in 4 out of 5 consecutive trials.

# Goal

Given each letter of the alphabet randomly, Michael will write the letter with correct line placement in 4 out of 5 consecutive trials on 3 occasions.

# Present Levels of Performance

Jessica comes to school without brushing her teeth, washing her face and brushing her hair because she is left alone to get ready in the morning for school. She can physically perform the tasks after they are modeled for her and with practice.

# Objectives

1. At school, Jessica will demonstrate that she can brush her teeth without assistance or a model on 5 out of 5 trials.

2. At school, Jessica will demonstrate that she can wash her face and brush her hair without assistance or a model on 5 out of 5 trials.

3. At school, Jessica will demonstrate that she can brush her teeth, wash her face and brush her hair without assistance or a model on 5 out of 5 trials.

# Goal

Jessica will come to school with her teeth brushed, her face washed and her hair brushed daily.

# Present Levels of Performance

Barry is unable to independently use his electric razor to shave. Barry does know what the electric razor looks like and can retrieve it on verbal request.

# Objectives

1. Barry will practice plugging in his razor to the wall outlet upon verbal request. Next Barry will turn on his razor upon verbal request. Finally, Barry will practice shaving his cheeks and chin with physical assistance. Barry will complete the plug-in and turning on razor with two or fewer verbal prompts.

2. Barry will independently plug in and turn on his electric razor when verbally prompted to shave. Barry will independently shave his cheeks and chin. Staff will provide physical assistance in showing Barry where he missed with the razor and help shave missed spots. Barry will complete this routine with no more than two prompts.

3. Barry will independently plug in and turn on his razor and shave his cheeks and chin. Barry will re-shave spots he missed with no more than one verbal prompt.

# Goal

Barry will independently locate his electric razor, plug it in, turn it on, and shave his chin and cheeks with no more than one verbal prompt.

# Present Levels of Performance

Frank is unable to ride the city bus to work independently. Frank has been riding the bus to work with his roommate.

# Objectives

1. Frank's job coach will make sure that Frank gets on bus 43 heading to the main station. Frank will complete this step with no more than one verbal reminder to check the bus number.

2. Frank will get on bus 43 without prompting and get off at the main bus station. He will then locate where to go to catch bus 38, the bus that will take Frank to his job. Frank will check the number on the bus to be sure that he is getting on bus 38. Frank will complete this routine with no more than one verbal reminder from his job coach.

3. Frank will get on bus 43 and transfer to bus 38 without error. Frank will be observed unobtrusively at the main station to make sure he is successful with the bus transfer.

# Goal

Frank will independently transport himself from home to work via city buses.

# Present Levels of Performance

Maurice forgets classroom assignments and fails to complete his homework half of the time.

# Objectives

1. Maurice will write down all of his class assignments in his memory book immediately after they are assigned. He will do this without error every day for a week.

2. Maurice will carry his memory book with him from home to school and home again every day for a week.

3. Maurice will use his memory book to remind him of his assignments so that he completes 75% of his homework assignments 4 out of 5 days.

# Goal

Maurice will complete all of his homework assignments, at least 3 out of 4 weeks each month.

# Present Levels of Performance

Ray is unable to open a combination lock without assistance. He understands the concept of lock, but he does not have the fine motor skills to turn the dial correctly. He recognizes two-digit numbers thru 100, and knows how to close a combination lock.

# Objectives

1. When given a combination lock, Ray will be able to grasp the spindle with his right hand on 4 out of 5 trials.

2. When given a combination lock, Ray will turn spindle to the correct digit of the first combination on 4 out of 5 trials.

3. When given a combination lock, Ray will be able to turn to the first and second digits of the combination correctly on 4 out of 5 trials.

# Goal

When given a combination lock with a combination number, Ray will be able to dial all three numbers of his lock combination correctly and open the lock independently on 4 out of 5 trials.

# Present Levels of Performance

In writing a persuasive paper, Ray's writing contains 1 of the 4 critical features for persuasive writing. He correctly uses indentation, capitalization, but not punctuation.

# Objectives

1. When writing a persuasive paper, Ray will begin with an opinion statement and use correct indentation, capitalization and punctuation.

2. When writing a persuasive paper, Ray will support his opinion statement with at least 3 facts and use correct indentation, capitalization and punctuation.

3. When writing a persuasive paper, Ray will finish the paper by reinstating opinion and use correct indentation, capitalization and punctuation.

# Goal

When writing persuasive essays, Ray's writing will contain all four of the critical features for persuasive writing as well as correct indentation, capitalization and punctuation on 3 out of 3 consecutive essays.

# Present Levels of Performance

Mike is a fifteen-year-old student who is training to work in his school library for class credit.

# Objectives

1. Given instructions on re-shelving books, Mike will be able to work independently on this task for the first fifteen minutes of each class session.

2. Given instructions on filing papers and cards, Mike will be able to work independently on this task for the second fifteen minutes of each class session.

3. Given instructions on garbage disposal and recycling techniques, Mike will be able to work independently on this task for the final fifteen minutes of the class session.

# Goal

When reminded of the above 3 daily tasks in the library, Mike will be able to work independently for the entire forty-five minute class period.

# Present Levels of Performance

Rick enjoys playing kick ball during P.E., but he will not run the bases after he kicks the ball (the coach allows students to run all the bases instead of stopping at each one, if the students are not developmentally ready for the typical rules of kick ball). He kicks the ball and then stands there. The coach tells him to run, but when he does not move, the coach asks him to step aside for the next player to kick.

# Objectives

1. During a kick ball game, after he kicks the ball, Rick will run the bases while holding the hand of a teammate, for 3 consecutive kick ball games.

2. During a kick ball game, after he kicks the ball, Rick will run the bases with a teammate running beside him without holding his hand, for 3 consecutive kick ball games.

3. During a kick ball game, after he kicks the ball, Rick will run the bases with a teammate running just to first base with him, for 3 consecutive kick ball games.

# Goal

During a kick ball game, Rick will run the bases after he kicks the ball.

# Present Levels of Performance

Paco is a high school junior who does not know how to initiate and implement a job search.

# Objectives

1. Paco will identify a list of 10 current job openings in the newspaper and 10 online that meet his interests and for which he is qualified.

2. Paco will legibly complete a sample job application with 100% accuracy.

3. Paco will participate in a mock interview with an 85% success rating in interviewer evaluation.

# Goal

Paco will identify 10 currently open jobs (with 100% accuracy), complete and submit an application for each (with 100% accuracy) and will participate in at least one interview.

# Present Levels of Performance

Mary is an 18 year old student who would like to live in her own apartment after leaving the public school system at age 21. Mary can currently put a cup of water into a microwave. Given a prompt, Mary knows how to open the microwave door and set the timer for 10, 30, 60 or 90 seconds in order to heat water to the necessary temperature.

# Objectives

1. Given a prompt, Mary will open the cupboard and take out a packet of cereal from an open box within 60 seconds for 4 out of 5 trials.

2. Having accessed a packet of cereal, Mary will independently tear open the top of the packet of cereal within 30 seconds for 4 out of 5 trials.

3. With an open packet of cereal, Mary will independently put it into a cup, add water to a marked line and microwave the cereal for 60 seconds.

# Goal

Mary will independently make hot cereal in a microwave for 4 out of 5 probes.

# Present Levels of Performance

Bob is a 10th grade student who is interested in the culinary arts and would like to become a chef when he graduates from high school in two years. A well-respected chef in town has told Bob that he needs to have a food handler's card in order to gain initial work experience in a restaurant.

# Objectives

1. Given a food handler's book and study guide, Bob will use the book to answer 18 out of 20 questions accurately.

2. Given visual cues in the school's kitchen, Bob will accurately answer questions about personal hygiene, food temperature and food storage.

3. Given a sample food handler's test, Bob will answer 18 out of 20 questions accurately.

# Goal

Bob will pass the food handler's test and earn his card by the end of the school year.

# Present Levels of Performance

Cassidy is a junior in high school who would like to attend the local community college when she graduates. Cassidy is a shy student who expresses concern at going to a new campus, meeting new people, and being able to find the buildings and the rooms that she will need to go to on campus.

# Objectives

1. Given an opportunity from her family or a high school field trip, Cassidy will attend a campus tour of the local community college.

2. Given a map of the community college campus, Cassidy will identify the main services (e.g., registrar, cafeteria, student services office, financial aid office, career counseling office, etc.) and main buildings that she would most likely use.

3. With a family member or friend, Cassidy will go to the campus and walk to the offices and buildings that she has identified on the campus map.

# Goal

Cassidy will independently visit the community college campus by the end of the year.

# Present Levels of Performance

Sam is a 15 years old. Sam does not know any activities he can engage in during free time in school or in the community. Currently, his interests are to eat and to sleep.

# Objectives

1. Sam will be taught at least one new leisure activity in his classroom each week for ten weeks.

2. With his class, Sam will participate in leisure activities in the community twice a month for 3 months.

3. Independently, Sam will choose at least one leisure activity in the community each week and one leisure activity at school each day for 3 months.

# Goal

Sam will initiate leisure activities at school and in the community on a weekly basis.

# Present Levels of Performance

Hank does not write down phone messages that are left at his place of employment. Often Hank hangs up the phone without listening to a call from a stranger because he is confused about how to take a message. Hank writes all his letters and numbers when his teacher dictates them, but he has not learned to spell.

# Objectives

1. Hank will locate writing materials both at school and at his job to use in recording a message.

2. In his classroom at school and using practice phones, Hank will ask the caller to spell out his/her name and ask for a phone number. Hank will record the name with two or fewer recorded letter errors and record the number with no errors.

3. At his job site, Hank will record the name and phone number of the caller during prearranged calls from his teacher with no more than one letter error and no number errors.

# Goal

Hank will record brief messages limited to name and phone number with no errors at his place of employment.

# Present Levels of Performance

Karen is a senior in high school. Karen types words dictated from an 8th grade list with 90% accuracy. Keyboarding is very time consuming and laborious for her. Karen has not been able to write letters of inquiry or correspond in writing with employers. Karen has excellent diction and uses well constructed sentences when she speaks. Karen uses a computer and spell checks regularly.

# Objectives

1. Karen will copy a twenty item handwritten grocery list using speech to print assistive technology (Dragon Naturally Speaking) and a spell check with no spelling errors.

2. Karen will read nine out of ten printed sentences into a new printed document using speech-to-print assistive technology without error. Sentences will begin with a capital letter and end with the proper punctuation mark and be spaced one line apart in her document.

3. Karen will construct a paragraph on a subject of her choosing which contains at least five sentences. The paragraph will be indented. Sentences will begin with a capital letter and end with the proper punctuation. The paragraphs will be checked by spell check and contain no spelling errors.

# Goal

Karen will write a letter of inquiry to an employer using a speech-to-print assistive technology program.

# Present Levels of Performance

Jason currently completes the reading assignments in his science textbook and answers chapter questions independently 25% of the time, with 50% accuracy on written portions.

# Objectives

1. Given a 250 word passage taken from his science textbook, Jason will read the passage in class and answer the even numbered chapter questions with 75% accuracy.

2. Given a full chapter from his science textbook, Jason will read the chapter in class and answer the even numbered chapter questions with 80% accuracy.

3. Given a full chapter from his science textbook, Jason will read the chapter at home and answer the even numbered chapter questions with 80% accuracy.

# Goal

Given a full chapter from his science textbook, Jason will read the chapter at home and answer all of the chapter questions with 90% accuracy.

# Present Levels of Performance

Erika is observed singing with peers in music class less than 10% of the time. She sits either in the corner or lays on the floor and has been observed crying and/or pinching herself in 13 of 17 music classes this year. The two days these behaviors were not observed, the music teacher had allowed Erica to put cotton balls in her ears to muffle the volume of noise in the room.

# Objectives

1. Given the opportunity to keep cotton balls in her ears, Erika will sit in music class while her peers are singing, within 2 feet of the group.

2. Given the opportunity to keep cotton balls in her ears, Erika will sit in music class, within 2 feet of the group, participating in either singing or tapping the beat on a drum 50% of the time.

3. Given the opportunity to keep cotton balls in her ears, Erika will sit in music class, within 2 feet of the group, participating in the same activity as the group 75% of the time.

# Goal

Given the opportunity to keep cotton balls in her ears to decrease the volume of the group, Erika will participate in music class 75% of the time.